Homestyle Cooking for Today

BRIMAR

Published in 1998 by
Brimar Publishing Inc.
338 Saint Antoine St. East
Montreal, Canada H2Y 1A3
Tel. (514) 954-1441
Fax (514) 954-5086

Photography: Nathalie Dumouchel
Food Stylist: Josée Robitaille
Graphic Design: Zapp
Props courtesy of: Stokes
Pier 1 Imports
Ramca
Regal Ware Inc.

Pictured on the front cover: *Ham 'n Veggie Pasta Dinner* (see recipe, page 61)

All recipes were developed and tested in the Land O'Lakes Test Kitchens.
Land O'Lakes Publications Manager: Mary Sue Peterson
Test Kitchen Coordinator: Cindy Manwarren

Design, photography and production by Brimar Publishing Inc.

ISBN 2-89433-418-4
Printed in Canada

Homestyle Cooking for Today

For over 75 years, Land O'Lakes has been a leader in providing the freshest and best dairy products. Now, with this wonderful collection of quick and delicious recipes, we are proud to present our best results – from our kitchen to yours.

Homestyle Cooking for Today features over 140 tried and tested recipes that are perfect for today's busy lifestyles. From simple soups and main dishes to delicious desserts, you'll find a variety of recipes for every taste and occasion.

Concise instructions along with preparation and cooking times make it easy for you to create a sensation in no time, while beautiful full-color photos and step-by-step techniques show you just what you get – fantastic meals for everyone to enjoy. Every recipe also includes facts on calories, protein, carbohydrates, fat, cholesterol and sodium.

So if you're looking for tasty, nutritious meals that are easy to prepare and sure to please, look no further. LAND O LAKES® *Homestyle Cooking for Today* has it all!

THE LAND O'LAKES STORY

Land O'Lakes was organized in 1921 by individuals who recognized the opportunity that marketing sweet cream butter could represent to Minnesota dairy farmers. By replacing the sour butter that was commonly available at the time with high quality sweet cream butter, the organization would increase farmers' income and improve the quality of their products. In 1924, the brand name LAND O LAKES was selected following a nationwide contest. From those early years, when the founders literally changed America's eating habits with the introduction of sweet cream butter, Land O'Lakes has grown into one of the best known, most respected and most successful food and agricultural businesses.

It wasn't long after Land O'Lakes achieved success marketing butter that the organization realized it might be able to do the same with other food products. The company has become firmly established as the premier dairy foods marketing cooperative, supplying a full line of dairy products – including butter, spreads, cheese and sour creams – to consumer, foodservice and specialty markets. In addition, the Land O'Lakes Test Kitchen serves as a valued source of appealing recipes for these popular dairy products.

Contents

Soups and Stews

MINESTRONE WITH PASTA

Preparation time: 15 minutes
Cooking time: 29 minutes

1¼ cups	uncooked dried ditalini *or* medium pasta shells	300 mL
1 tbsp	butter	15 mL
1	medium onion, chopped	1
¼ cup	chopped fresh basil leaves*	50 mL
1 tsp	finely chopped fresh garlic	5 mL
1 lb	chorizo *or* Italian sausage, crumbled	450 g
2	medium carrots, sliced	2
2	medium zucchini, cut into ½-inch (1 cm) pieces	2
1	can (14 oz/397g) whole tomatoes, cut up	1
1	package (9 oz/255 g) frozen cut green beans	1
4	cans (14½ oz/429 mL each) beef broth	4
	Freshly grated Parmesan cheese	

- Cook ditalini according to package directions. Drain. Set aside.
- Meanwhile, in Dutch oven, melt butter until sizzling; add onion, basil and garlic. Cook over medium-high heat, stirring constantly, until onion is softened (3 to 5 minutes). Add sausage. Continue cooking, stirring occasionally, until sausage is browned (9 to 11 minutes). Drain off fat.
- Stir in all remaining ingredients *except* Parmesan cheese. Continue cooking, stirring occasionally, until vegetables are crisply tender (15 to 20 minutes). Stir in cooked ditalini. Continue cooking, stirring occasionally, until heated through (2 to 3 minutes). Sprinkle each serving with Parmesan cheese.

* *Substitute 2 tsp (10 mL) dried basil leaves.*

8 servings

NUTRITION FACTS (1 serving)
Calories 380 • Protein 20 g • Carbohydrate 20 g
Fat 24 g • Cholesterol 50 mg • Sodium 1460 mg

VEGETARIAN THREE-BEAN CHILI

Preparation time: 20 minutes
Cooking time: 49 minutes

1 tbsp	butter	15 mL
1	large onion, chopped	1
1	medium green pepper, chopped	1
1 tsp	finely chopped fresh garlic	5 mL
3 cups	water	750 mL
1 cup	dried lentils	250 mL
1	can (28 oz/794 g) whole tomatoes, undrained, cut up	1
1	can (8 oz/237 mL) tomato sauce	1
2 tbsp	chili powder	30 mL
2 tsp	ground cumin	10 mL
1 tsp	dried oregano leaves	5 mL
½ tsp	salt	2 mL
1	can (15½ oz/439 g) kidney beans, rinsed, drained	1
1	can (15 oz/425 g) great Northern beans, drained	1
	Shredded Cheddar cheese, if desired	
	Jalapeño pepper slices, if desired	

- In large saucepan, melt butter until sizzling; add onion, green pepper and garlic. Cook over medium-high heat, stirring occasionally, until vegetables are crisply tender (3 to 5 minutes).
- Stir in water and lentils. Continue cooking until mixture comes to a full boil (4 to 6 minutes). Reduce heat to low. Cook until lentils are tender (25 to 30 minutes).
- Stir in all remaining ingredients *except* beans, cheese and jalapeños. Continue cooking until slightly thickened and flavors are blended (15 to 20 minutes).
- Stir in beans; continue cooking until heated through (2 to 4 minutes). Serve with cheese and jalapeños, if desired.

8 servings

NUTRITION FACTS (1 serving)
Calories 230 • Protein 14 g • Carbohydrate 39 g
Fat 3 g • Cholesterol 0 mg • Sodium 490 mg

CREAMY CHICKEN AND ORZO SOUP

***Preparation time:* 7 minutes**
***Cooking time:* 25 minutes**

2 tbsp	butter	30 mL
1 cup	coarsely chopped carrots	250 mL
½ cup	coarsely chopped celery	125 mL
¼ cup	chopped green onion	50 mL
1 cup	uncooked dried rosamarina pasta (orzo)	250 mL
2	cans (14½ oz/429 mL each) low-sodium chicken broth	2
1½ tsp	dried Italian seasoning*	7 mL
¼ tsp	salt	1 mL
⅛ tsp	pepper	0.5 mL
1½ cups	milk	375 mL
2 tbsp	all-purpose flour	30 mL
2 cups	finely chopped cooked chicken	500 mL

- In large saucepan, melt butter until sizzling; add carrots, celery and green onion. Cook over medium-high heat until vegetables are crisply tender (5 to 6 minutes).
- Stir in rosamarina, chicken broth, Italian seasoning, salt and pepper. Continue cooking until mixture comes to a full boil (4 to 5 minutes). Reduce heat to low; cook 5 minutes.
- In small bowl stir together milk and flour until smooth. Add to soup, stirring constantly, until mixture comes to a boil and is slightly thickened (2 to 3 minutes). Add chicken and cook until heated through.

TIP: If soup becomes too thick, stir in additional milk.

** Substitute ½ tsp (2 mL) each dried oregano, marjoram and basil leaves, and ⅛ tsp (0.5 mL) rubbed sage.*

4 servings

NUTRITION FACTS (1 serving)
Calories 440 • Protein 31 g • Carbohydrate 46 g
Fat 15 g • Cholesterol 80 mg • Sodium 810 mg

Savory sausage stew

Preparation time: 15 minutes
Cooking time: 30 minutes

½ lb	kielbasa *or* smoked sausage, cut into ½-inch (1 cm) pieces	225 g
2	medium carrots, sliced ¼-inch (5 mm)	2
1	stalk celery, sliced ½-inch (1 cm)	1
1	medium onion, chopped	1
2 cups	coleslaw	500 mL
¼ cup	chopped parsley	50 mL
2	cans (14½ oz/429 mL each) Italian *or* plum-style diced tomatoes	2
¼ tsp	salt	1 mL
⅛ tsp	pepper	0.5 mL

- In Dutch oven, combine kielbasa, carrots, celery and onion. Cook over medium heat, stirring occasionally, until vegetables are crisply tender (8 to 12 minutes).
- Add all remaining ingredients. Continue cooking, stirring occasionally, until mixture comes to a full boil (2 to 3 minutes). Reduce heat to low. Cook until vegetables are tender (20 to 25 minutes).

4 servings

NUTRITION FACTS (1 serving)
Calories 290 • Protein 13 g • Carbohydrate 26 g
Fat 16 g • Cholesterol 40 mg • Sodium 1450 mg

BROCCOLI CHEESE SOUP

Preparation time: 20 minutes
Cooking time: 22 minutes

1 cup	uncooked dried gemelli (double twist pasta) *or* rotini (corkscrew *or* pasta twists)	250 mL
2 cups	broccoli florets*	500 mL
¼ cup	butter	50 mL
½ cup	sliced leeks, ⅛-inch (3 mm)	125 mL
1 tbsp	finely chopped shallots**	15 mL
3 tbsp	all-purpose flour	45 mL
¼ tsp	dry mustard	1 mL
¼ tsp	coarsely ground pepper	1 mL
2	medium carrots, shredded	2
2	cans (14½ oz/429 mL each) low-sodium chicken broth	2
1 tsp	Worcestershire sauce	5 mL
1 cup	half-and-half *or* milk	250 mL
1½ cups	shredded sharp Cheddar cheese	375 mL

- Cook gemelli according to package directions, adding broccoli during last 6 minutes of cooking time. Drain. Set aside.
- Meanwhile, in Dutch oven, melt butter until sizzling; add leeks and shallots. Cook over medium heat, stirring occasionally, until softened (3 to 5 minutes).
- Stir in flour, mustard and pepper. Continue cooking, stirring constantly, until bubbly (1 minute). Add carrots, chicken broth and Worcestershire sauce. Continue cooking, stirring occasionally, until soup just comes to a boil (3 to 5 minutes).
- Add half-and-half. Continue cooking, stirring occasionally, until heated through (2 to 4 minutes). Add cheese. Continue cooking, stirring constantly, until cheese is melted (1 to 2 minutes).
- Add cooked gemelli and broccoli. Continue cooking until heated through (3 to 5 minutes).

** Substitute 1 package (10 oz/284 g) chopped frozen broccoli, thawed. But do not cook broccoli with gemelli. Add to soup when gemelli is added.*

*** Substitute 1 tbsp (15 mL) chopped onion.*

6 servings

NUTRITION FACTS (1 serving)
Calories 350 • Protein 14 g • Carbohydrate 24 g
Fat 22 g • Cholesterol 65 mg • Sodium 330 mg

GARDEN ABC SOUP

Preparation time: 20 minutes
Cooking time: 47 minutes

2 tsp	butter	10 mL
1	medium onion, chopped	1
½ tsp	finely chopped fresh garlic	2 mL
½ cup	dried lentils	125 mL
1 cup	water	250 mL
3	cans (14½ oz/429 mL each) low-sodium chicken broth	3
2	large carrots, thinly sliced	2
2	medium red potatoes, cubed ½-inch (1 cm)	2
½ tsp	dried marjoram leaves	2 mL
½ tsp	dried tarragon leaves	2 mL
⅛ tsp	coarsely ground pepper	0.5 mL
1 cup	frozen peas	250 mL
½ cup	uncooked dried rosamarina pasta (orzo) *or* small pasta shells	125 mL
1	can (14½ oz/429 mL) diced tomatoes	1

- In large saucepan, melt butter until sizzling; add onion and garlic. Cook over medium heat, stirring occasionally, until onion is softened (3 to 5 minutes).
- Add all remaining ingredients *except* peas, rosamarina and tomatoes. Cook over high heat until mixture comes to a full boil (6 to 8 minutes).
- Reduce heat to low. Cover and cook until lentils and potatoes are tender (20 to 25 minutes).
- Add peas, rosamarina and tomatoes. Increase heat to high. Cook until mixture comes to a full boil (8 to 10 minutes). Reduce heat to low. Cook until pasta is tender (10 to 12 minutes).

TIP: When preparing lentils with acidic ingredients like tomatoes, do not add tomatoes until lentils are cooked as desired.

8 servings

NUTRITION FACTS (1 serving)
Calories 130 • Protein 8 g • Carbohydrate 21 g
Fat 1 g • Cholesterol <5mg • Sodium 170 mg

1

Cook onion and garlic over medium heat, stirring occasionally, until softened.

2

Add all remaining ingredients except peas, rosamarina and tomatoes.

3

Add peas, rosamarina and tomatoes.

Potato and Corn Chowder

Preparation time: 10 minutes
Cooking time: 10 minutes

3 tbsp	butter	45 mL
1	medium onion, chopped	1
3 tbsp	all-purpose flour	45 mL
¼ tsp	salt	1 mL
¼ tsp	pepper	1 mL
3 cups	milk *or* half-and-half	750 mL
1	can (15 oz/425 g) whole potatoes, quartered	1
1	can (11 oz/312 g) whole kernel corn with red and green peppers	1
	Shredded Cheddar cheese, if desired	
	Parsley, if desired	
	Hot pepper sauce, if desired	

- In large saucepan, melt butter until sizzling; add onion. Cook over medium heat, stirring occasionally, until softened (4 to 5 minutes).
- Stir in flour, salt and pepper until bubbly (1 minute). With wire whisk, stir in milk. Continue cooking, stirring occasionally, until mixture comes to a full boil (2 to 3 minutes). Boil 1 minute.
- Stir in potatoes and corn. Continue cooking, stirring occasionally, until heated through (3 to 4 minutes).
- To serve, ladle into individual bowls. Top with cheese, parsley and hot sauce, if desired.

4 servings

NUTRITION FACTS (1 serving)
Calories 300 • Protein 10 g • Carbohydrate 38 g
Fat 13 g • Cholesterol 35 mg • Sodium 920 mg

Potato Black Bean Soup

Preparation time: 15 minutes
Cooking time: 21 minutes

6 cups	vegetable *or* chicken broth	1.5 L
8 oz	mushrooms, quartered	225 g
4	medium potatoes, peeled, cut into 1-inch (2.5 cm) cubes	4
1	medium onion, chopped	1
1	can (15 oz/425 g) black beans, rinsed, drained	1
1	can (14½ oz/411 g) whole tomatoes, cut up	1
2 tbsp	chopped fresh cilantro	30 mL
1 tbsp	Cajun seasoning	15 mL
½ cup	fat free sour cream	125 mL

- In large saucepan, stir together broth, mushrooms, potatoes and onion. Cook over medium-high heat, stirring occasionally, until mixture just comes to a boil (8 to 10 minutes). Reduce heat to medium. Cover and cook, stirring occasionally, until potatoes are just tender (10 to 12 minutes).
- Stir in all remaining ingredients *except* sour cream. Continue cooking, stirring occasionally, until heated through (3 to 5 minutes).
- To serve, ladle into individual bowls. Dollop with sour cream.

8 servings

NUTRITION FACTS (1 serving)
Calories 150 • Protein 7 g • Carbohydrate 30 g
Fat 1 g • Cholesterol 0 mg • Sodium 1050 mg

BEAN AND VEGETABLE STEW

Preparation time: 10 minutes
Cooking time: 20 minutes

1 tbsp	vegetable oil	15 mL
4	medium carrots, sliced ¼-inch (5 mm)	4
1	medium red onion, cut into ½-inch (1 cm) pieces	1
1	medium green pepper, cut into 1-inch (2.5 cm) pieces	1
1 tsp	dried thyme leaves	5 mL
1 tsp	rubbed sage	5 mL
¼ tsp	salt	1 mL
¼ tsp	coarsely ground pepper	1 mL
1 tsp	finely chopped fresh garlic	5 mL
1	can (15½ oz/439 g) pinto beans, undrained	1
1	can (15 oz/425 g) great Northern beans, undrained	1
1	can (14½ oz /411 g) Mexican-style stewed tomatoes	1

- In large saucepan, heat oil; add all remaining ingredients *except* beans, tomatoes and cheese. Cook over medium-high heat, stirring occasionally, until vegetables are browned and very tender (12 to 15 minutes).
- Stir in beans and tomatoes. Continue cooking, stirring occasionally, until heated through (8 to 10 minutes). Serve with shredded Monterey Jack cheese, if desired.

6 servings

NUTRITION FACTS (1 serving)
Calories 180 • Protein 9 g • Carbohydrate 33 g
Fat 3 g • Cholesterol 0 mg • Sodium 230 mg

Macaroni and Cheese Chowder

Preparation time: 20 minutes
Cooking time: 13 minutes

1 cup	uncooked dried elbow macaroni *or* gemelli (double twist pasta)	250 mL
2 tbsp	butter	30 mL
¼ cup	coarsely chopped onion	50 mL
1	medium carrot, coarsely chopped	1
1	stalk celery, coarsely chopped	1
¼ cup	all-purpose flour	50 mL
½ tsp	dry mustard	2 mL
½ tsp	salt	2 mL
3 cups	milk	750 mL
1 cup	chicken broth	250 mL
2 cups	shredded American cheese	500 mL

- Cook macaroni according to package directions. Drain. Set aside.
- Meanwhile, in large saucepan, melt butter until sizzling; add onion, carrot and celery. Cook over medium heat, stirring occasionally, until vegetables are crisply tender (3 to 5 minutes).
- Stir in flour, mustard and salt. Continue cooking, stirring constantly, until bubbly (1 minute). Stir in milk and chicken broth. Continue cooking, stirring occasionally, until mixture comes to a full boil (8 to 12 minutes). Boil 1 minute.
- Stir in cooked macaroni and cheese. Continue cooking, stirring occasionally, until cheese is melted (1 to 2 minutes).

5 servings

NUTRITION FACTS (1 serving)
Calories 370 • Protein 18 g • Carbohydrate 27 g
Fat 21 g • Cholesterol 60 mg • Sodium 1020 mg

CHUNKY CHICKEN CHILI

Preparation time: 15 minutes
Cooking time: 58 minutes

3 cups	cubed cooked boneless skinless chicken breast	750 mL
4 cups	chicken broth *or* water	1 L
1	can (28 oz/794 g) whole tomatoes, cut up	1
1	can (15 oz/425 g) black beans, rinsed, drained	1
1	can (15½ oz/439 g) pinto beans, rinsed, drained	1
1	can (4 oz/113 g) chopped mild green chilies, drained	1
1	medium onion, chopped	1
1 tbsp	chili powder	15 mL
1 tbsp	ground cumin	15 mL
½ tsp	crushed red pepper	2 mL

- In Dutch oven, combine all ingredients. Cook over medium-high heat until mixture comes to a full boil (8 to 10 minutes).
- Reduce heat to low. Cook, stirring occasionally, until slightly thickened (50 to 60 minutes).

10 servings

NUTRITION FACTS (1 serving)
Calories 210 • Protein 21 g • Carbohydrate 18 g
Fat 6 g • Cholesterol 40 mg • Sodium 920 mg

QUICK TACO SOUP

Preparation time: 20 minutes
Cooking time: 10 minutes

½ lb	extra lean ground beef	225 g
2	medium onions, chopped	2
1	large green pepper, chopped	1
1	package (1.25 oz/35 g) taco seasoning mix	1
4 cups	vegetable tomato juice	1 L
1½ cups	thick and chunky salsa *or* picante sauce	375 mL
	Fat free sour cream, if desired	
	Shredded lettuce, sliced green onions, chopped tomato *and/or* shredded Cheddar cheese, if desired	

- In large saucepan, cook ground beef, onions and green pepper over medium-high heat, stirring occasionally, until beef is no longer pink (6 to 10 minutes). Drain off fat.
- Stir in seasoning mix; continue cooking 1 minute. Stir in tomato juice and salsa. Continue cooking, stirring occasionally, until heated through (3 to 5 minutes).
- To serve, ladle soup into individual bowls. Dollop with sour cream, if desired. Top with your choice of your toppings.

8 servings

NUTRITION FACTS (1 serving)
Calories 110 • Protein 7 g • Carbohydrate 13 g
Fat 4 g • Cholesterol 20 mg • Sodium 950 mg

QUICK FRENCH ONION SOUP

Preparation time: 15 minutes
Cooking time: 16 minutes
Broiling time: 2 minutes

1 tbsp	butter	15 mL
2¾ cups	water	675 mL
3	medium onions, thinly sliced	3
1 tsp	finely chopped fresh garlic	5 mL
2	cans (10½ oz/310 mL each) beef consomme	2
¼ tsp	pepper	1 mL
1 cup	seasoned croutons	250 mL
8	slices Swiss cheese	8
1 tbsp	chopped fresh parsley	15 mL

- In large saucepan, melt butter until sizzling; add *¼ cup (50 mL)* water, onions and garlic. Cook over high heat, stirring occasionally, until onions are softened and lightly browned (6 to 8 minutes).
- Add remaining 2½ cups (625 mL) water, beef consomme and pepper. Reduce heat to medium. Continue cooking 10 minutes.
- Meanwhile, *heat broiler*. Ladle soup into 4 ovenproof bowls. Sprinkle each with *¼ cup (50 mL)* croutons; top with *2 slices* cheese. Place bowls on 15 x 10 x 1-inch (37.5 x 25 x 2.5 cm) jelly roll pan for easier handling.
- Broil 5 to 6 inches (13 to 15 cm) from heat until cheese is melted (2 to 3 minutes). Sprinkle with parsley.

4 servings

NUTRITION FACTS (1 serving)
Calories 190 • Protein 10 g • Carbohydrate 10 g
Fat 12 g • Cholesterol 30 mg • Sodium 630 mg

CHINESE NOODLE AND PORK SOUP

Preparation time: 15 minutes
Cooking time: 5 minutes

2 oz	uncooked Chinese egg noodles*	60 g
2 cups	thinly sliced Chinese cabbage**	500 mL
1½ cups	cubed cooked pork	375 mL
¼ cup	chopped green onions	50 mL
2	cans (14½ oz/429 mL each) low-sodium chicken broth	2
1	can (4 oz/113 g) mushroom pieces and stems, undrained	1
1 tsp	finely chopped fresh gingerroot	5 mL
¼ tsp	crushed red pepper flakes	1 mL
	Chopped green onions, if desired	

- Cook egg noodles according to package directions. Drain.
- Meanwhile, in large saucepan, combine all remaining ingredients. Stir in cooked noodles. Bring to a full boil over high heat (5 to 8 minutes).
- To serve, ladle soup into individual bowls. Sprinkle each serving with chopped green onions, if desired.

** Substitute 2 oz (60 g) fine egg noodles or vermicelli.*

*** Substitute 2 cups (500 mL) shredded cabbage.*

4 servings

NUTRITION FACTS (1 serving)
Calories 220 • Protein 23 g • Carbohydrate 15 g
Fat 7 g • Cholesterol 60 mg • Sodium 270 mg

Stir in flour, salt, pepper and allspice. Continue cooking, stirring constantly, until mixture is bubbly.

Add broth and turkey. Continue cooking, stirring constantly, until mixture comes to a full boil.

Stir in milk and wild rice. Continue cooking until heated through.

TURKEY AND WILD RICE SOUP

Preparation time: 20 minutes
Cooking time: 11 minutes

6 tbsp	butter	90 mL
½ cup	chopped carrots	125 mL
½ cup	chopped celery	125 mL
½ cup	chopped onion	125 mL
⅓ cup	all-purpose flour	75 mL
½ tsp	salt	2 mL
¼ tsp	pepper	1 mL
⅛ tsp	allspice	0.5 mL
1	can (14½ oz /429 mL) chicken broth	1
1 cup	chopped cooked turkey	250 mL
2 cups	milk *or* half-and-half	500 mL
1½ cups	cooked wild rice	375 mL
	Chopped fresh parsley, if desired	

- In large saucepan, melt butter until sizzling; add carrots, celery and onion. Cook over medium heat until vegetables are crisply tender (4 to 5 minutes).
- Stir in flour, salt, pepper and allspice. Continue cooking, stirring constantly, until mixture is bubbly (1 to 2 minutes). Add broth and turkey. Continue cooking, stirring constantly, until mixture comes to a full boil (2 to 3 minutes). Boil 1 minute.
- Stir in milk and wild rice. Continue cooking until heated through (2 to 5 minutes). Garnish with chopped fresh parsley, if desired.

5 servings

NUTRITION FACTS (1 serving)
Calories 320 • Protein 17g • Carbohydrate 25g
Fat 18 g • Cholesterol 65 mg • Sodium 700 mg

Poultry

Lemon Chicken Sauté

Preparation time: 20 minutes
Cooking time: 9 minutes

6	boneless skinless chicken breasts (4 oz/115 g each)	6
2 tbsp	butter	30 mL
1 tsp	finely chopped fresh garlic	5 mL
¼ tsp	salt	1 mL
⅛ tsp	pepper	0.5 mL
2 tbsp	lemon juice	30 mL
1 cup	sliced green onions, 1 inch (2.5 cm)	250 mL
1 cup	fresh mushrooms, halved	250 mL
	Lemon slices, if desired	
	Fresh parsley, if desired	

- Flatten each chicken breast to about ¼-inch (5 mm) thickness by pounding between sheets of waxed paper.
- In large skillet, melt butter until sizzling; add chicken breasts, garlic, salt and pepper. Cook over medium heat, turning once, until no longer pink (10 to 12 minutes). Place chicken on serving platter; keep warm.
- Stir lemon juice into pan drippings. Add green onions and mushrooms. Continue cooking, stirring constantly, until heated through (2 to 3 minutes). Spoon over chicken. Garnish with lemon slices and parsley, if desired.

6 servings

NUTRITION FACTS (1 serving)
Calories 170 • Protein 25 g • Carbohydrate 2 g
Fat 7 g • Cholesterol 75 mg • Sodium 190 mg

Saucy Sweet and Sour Meatballs

Preparation time: 20 minutes
Cooking time: 37 minutes

MEATBALLS

½ cup	fine dry bread crumbs	125 mL
1½ lbs	lean ground fresh turkey*	675 g
1	medium onion, finely chopped	1
2 tbsp	soy sauce	30 mL
1	egg, beaten	1
1 tsp	finely chopped fresh garlic	5 mL
2 tbsp	vegetable oil	30 mL

SAUCE

	Orange juice	
1	can (8 oz/227 g) pineapple chunks in juice, drained, *juice reserved*	1
¼ cup	firmly packed brown sugar	50 mL
¼ cup	vinegar	50 mL
1	medium carrot, sliced	1
½ tsp	salt	2 mL
½ tsp	finely chopped fresh garlic	2 mL
2 tsp	soy sauce	10 mL
1 tbsp	cornstarch	15 mL
2 tbsp	cold water	30 mL
½	medium green pepper, cut into 1-inch (2.5 cm) pieces	½
	Hot cooked couscous	

- In medium bowl, lightly mix together all meatball ingredients *except* oil. Shape into twelve 2-inch (5 cm) balls.
- In large skillet, heat oil; add meatballs. Cook over medium heat, turning occasionally, until browned (10 to 15 minutes). Remove from skillet; keep warm.
- Add enough orange juice to pineapple juice to equal ¾ cup (175 mL). In same skillet, place juice, brown sugar, vinegar, carrot, salt, garlic and soy sauce. Cook over medium heat until mixture just comes to a boil (2 to 5 minutes). Reduce heat to low. Cover and cook until carrots are crisply tender (5 to 7 minutes).
- In small bowl, combine cornstarch and cold water; stir into sauce in skillet. Cook until mixture just comes to a boil (2 to 3 minutes).
- Add meatballs, pineapple and green pepper. Cook over medium heat, stirring occasionally, until mixture just comes to a boil (8 to 10 minutes). Reduce heat to low. Cook until meatballs are no longer pink (10 to 15 minutes). Serve with couscous.

** Substitute 1½ lbs (675 g) lean ground beef or chicken.*

6 servings

NUTRITION FACTS (1 serving)
Calories 340 • Protein 23 g • Carbohydrate 27 g
Fat 15 g • Cholesterol 125 mg • Sodium 830 mg

MUSHROOM AND HERB CHICKEN DINNER

Preparation time: 10 minutes
Cooking time: 1 hour

3–4 lb	frying chicken, cut into 8 pieces, skinned	1.3 to 1.8 kg
2 tbsp	Roasted Garlic Butter with Olive Oil*	30 mL
1	can (10¾ oz/318 mL) condensed reduced fat cream of chicken *or* mushroom soup	1
1 tsp	chopped fresh rosemary leaves**	5 mL
1 tsp	chopped fresh thyme leaves**	5 mL
¼ cup	light *or* fat free sour cream	50 mL
2	cans (4 oz/113 g each) mushroom stems and pieces, drained	2
	Hot cooked noodles *or* rice	

- In large skillet, melt garlic butter until sizzling; add chicken. Cook over medium heat, turning occasionally, until chicken is browned (13 to 15 minutes).
- Push chicken pieces to one side of pan; stir in soup, rosemary and thyme until smooth. Reduce heat to low. Cover and cook, stirring occasionally, until chicken is no longer pink (45 to 55 minutes).
- Stir in sour cream and mushrooms; continue cooking until heated through (2 to 3 minutes). Serve over noodles or rice.

** Substitute 2 tbsp (30 mL) butter and 2 tsp (10 mL) finely chopped fresh garlic.*

*** Substitute ¼ tsp dried rosemary or thyme leaves.*

6 servings

NUTRITION FACTS (1 serving without noodles)
Calories 360 • Protein 51 g • Carbohydrate 7 g
Fat 13 g • Cholesterol 175 mg • Sodium 770 mg

QUICK TURKEY SAUTÉ

Preparation time: 10 minutes
Cooking time: 10 minutes

1 tbsp	butter	15 mL
1 lb	turkey tenderloin, cut into 1-inch (2.5 cm) pieces	450 g
1½ tsp	purchased minced garlic	7 mL
1½ cups	low-sodium chicken broth	375 mL
8 oz	sliced fresh mushrooms	225 g
5	green onions, cut into 1-inch (2.5 cm) pieces	5
4	Roma tomatoes, halved lengthwise, sliced crosswise	4
	Salt	
	Pepper	
	Hot cooked rice, if desired	

- In large skillet, melt butter until sizzling; add turkey pieces and garlic. Cook over medium-high heat, stirring occasionally, until turkey is no longer pink (4 to 5 minutes). Remove turkey from skillet; keep warm.
- Add broth, mushrooms and green onions to skillet. Cover and continue cooking, stirring occasionally, for 5 minutes.
- Add cooked turkey and tomatoes. Continue cooking until heated through (1 to 2 minutes). Season with salt and pepper to taste. Serve with hot cooked rice, if desired.

4 servings

NUTRITION FACTS (1 serving)
Calories 200 • Protein 31 g • Carbohydrate 7 g
Fat 4.5 g • Cholesterol 80 mg • Sodium 270 mg

CHICKEN 'N POTATO PAPRIKA

Preparation time: 20 minutes
Cooking time: 55 minutes

3 tbsp	butter	45 mL
3–4 lb	frying chicken, cut into 8 pieces	1.3 to 1.8 kg
1 tbsp	paprika	15 mL
2 tsp	instant chicken bouillon granules	10 mL
½ tsp	salt	2 mL
½ tsp	garlic powder	2 mL
⅛ tsp	pepper	0.5 mL
1	medium onion, sliced ⅛-inch (3 mm), separated into rings	1
1¼ cups	apple juice	300 mL
4	medium potatoes, peeled, quartered	4
4	medium carrots, sliced ¼-inch (5 mm) thick	4
1 cup	light sour cream	250 mL
2 tbsp	all-purpose flour	30 mL
2 tbsp	chopped fresh chives	30 mL

- In large skillet, melt butter until sizzling; add chicken. Cook over medium heat, turning occasionally, until browned (13 to 15 minutes).
- Sprinkle with paprika, bouillon granules, salt, garlic powder and pepper; top with onion rings. Add apple juice.
- Reduce heat to low. Cover and cook 15 minutes. Add potatoes and carrots. Cover and continue cooking until chicken is no longer pink and potatoes and carrots are fork tender (25 to 35 minutes).
- In small bowl, stir together sour cream, flour and chives. Push chicken and vegetables to one side of skillet. Stir sour cream mixture into liquid in skillet until well mixed. Carefully stir chicken and vegetables into sauce. Continue cooking, stirring occasionally, until thickened and heated through (2 to 3 minutes).

6 servings

NUTRITION FACTS (1 serving)
Calories 710 • Protein 46 g • Carbohydrate 34 g
Fat 42 g • Cholesterol 230 mg • Sodium 680 mg

Cook chicken over medium heat, turning occasionally, until browned.

Sprinkle with paprika, bouillon granules, salt, garlic powder and pepper; top with onion rings.

Add apple juice.

Add potatoes and carrots.

Stir together sour cream, flour and chives.

Stir sour cream mixture into liquid in skillet until well mixed. Carefully stir chicken and vegetables into sauce.

Dijon Sauced Chicken Breasts

Preparation time: 10 minutes
Cooking time: 15 minutes

2 tbsp	butter	30 mL
6	boneless skinless chicken breasts (5 oz/140 g each)	6
1 cup	sour cream (regular, light *or* fat free)	250 mL
⅓ cup	milk	75 mL
2 tbsp	Dijon-style mustard	30 mL
¼ cup	sliced green onions	50 mL

- In large skillet, melt butter until sizzling; add chicken breasts. Cook over medium-high heat, turning once, until chicken is no longer pink (12 to 15 minutes). Remove chicken from skillet; set aside.
- In same skillet, add sour cream, milk and mustard. Continue cooking, stirring constantly, until sauce is smooth and heated through (1 to 2 minutes).
- To serve, spoon sauce over chicken; sprinkle with green onions.

6 servings

NUTRITION FACTS (1 serving)
Calories 290 • Protein 35 g • Carbohydrate 4 g
Fat 14 g • Cholesterol 115 mg • Sodium 290 mg

Grilled Garlic Chicken

Preparation time: 15 minutes
Grilling time: 40 minutes

SAUCE

¼ cup	butter, melted	50 mL
3 tbsp	finely chopped fresh garlic	45 mL
2 tbsp	soy sauce	30 mL
¼ tsp	pepper	1 mL

CHICKEN

3–4 lb	frying chicken, cut into 8 pieces	1.3 to 1.8 kg
¼ cup	chopped fresh parsley	50 mL

- Heat gas grill to medium *or* charcoal grill until coals are ash white. Make aluminum foil drip pan; place opposite coals. In small bowl, stir together all sauce ingredients.
- Place chicken pieces on grill over drip pan; brush with sauce. Cover and grill, turning and brushing occasionally with sauce, until chicken is no longer pink (40 to 50 minutes). Sprinkle with parsley.

4 servings

NUTRITION FACTS (1 serving)
Calories 300 • Protein 41 g • Carbohydrate 1 g
Fat 13 g • Cholesterol 135 mg • Sodium 280 mg

SOUTH OF THE BORDER CHICKEN FAJITAS

Preparation time: 15 minutes
Marinating time: 1 hour
Broiling time: 8 minutes
Cooking time: 6 minutes

6	**boneless skinless chicken breasts (4 oz/115 g each), cut into ½-inch (1 cm) strips**	**6**
¾ cup	**purchased fajita marinade**	**175 mL**
1	**medium green pepper, cut into ¼-inch (5 mm) strips**	**1**
1	**medium red pepper, cut into ¼-inch (5 mm) strips**	**1**
1	**medium onion, sliced ¼-inch (5 mm), separated into rings**	**1**
1 tbsp	**vegetable oil**	**15 mL**
6	**8-inch (20 cm) flour tortillas, warmed**	**6**
2 cups	**shredded Cheddar cheese**	**500 mL**
	Salsa, if desired	

- In large resealable plastic food bag, place chicken and *½ cup (125 mL)* fajita marinade. Tightly seal bag. Turn bag several times to coat chicken well. Place in 13 x 9-inch (33 x 23 cm) pan. Refrigerate, turning occasionally, at least 1 hour. With slotted spoon, remove chicken from marinade; *discard marinade*.
- *Heat broiler.* Spray broiler pan with no stick cooking spray. Place peppers and onion on prepared pan; brush with *2 tbsp (30 mL)* fajita marinade. Broil 3 to 4 inches (7.5 to 10 cm) from heat until lightly browned and crisply tender (8 to 10 minutes). Set aside.
- Meanwhile, in large skillet, heat oil; add chicken. Cook over medium-high heat, stirring occasionally, until chicken is no longer pink (5 to 7 minutes). Add vegetables and remaining 2 tbsp (30 mL) marinade. Continue cooking until vegetables are heated through (1 to 2 minutes).
- To serve, divide chicken mixture evenly among tortillas; sprinkle each with *¼ cup (50 mL)* cheese. Fold tortilla edges over filling. Serve with remaining cheese and salsa, if desired.

6 servings

NUTRITION FACTS (1 serving)
Calories 460 • Protein 37 g • Carbohydrate 28 g
Fat 21 g • Cholesterol 105 mg • Sodium 585 mg

CHEESY ROSEMARY TURKEY BAKE

Preparation time: 20 minutes
Baking time: 45 minutes

6 cups	cubed cooked turkey	1.5 L
1 cup	mayonnaise	250 mL
¼ cup	slivered almonds	50 mL
6	stalks celery, sliced ½-inch (1 cm)	6
2 cups	shredded Cheddar *or* Chedarella® cheese	500 mL
1	medium onion, chopped	1
2 tbsp	lemon juice	30 mL
1 tsp	dried rosemary leaves, crushed	5 mL
½ tsp	salt	2 mL
½ tsp	pepper	2 mL

- Heat oven to 350°F (180°C). In large bowl, stir together all ingredients *except ½ cup (125 mL)* cheese. Spoon into large greased casserole or 13 x 9-inch (33 x 23 cm) baking pan.
- Cover and bake for 45 to 55 minutes or until heated through.
- Sprinkle with remaining cheese. Continue baking until cheese is melted (5 minutes).

TIP: To make ahead, prepare recipe as directed. Cover with plastic food wrap; refrigerate overnight. Remove plastic food wrap. Bake for 55 to 65 minutes or until heated through. Sprinkle with remaining cheese. Continue baking until cheese is melted (5 minutes).

8 servings

NUTRITION FACTS (1 serving)
Calories 510 • Protein 39 g • Carbohydrate 5 g
Fat 37 g • Cholesterol 120 mg • Sodium 600 mg

SKILLET CHICKEN ITALIANO

Preparation time: 15 minutes
Cooking time: 26 minutes

6 oz	uncooked dried fettuccine	170 g
2 tbsp	butter	30 mL
1 tbsp	dried Italian seasoning	15 mL
4	boneless skinless chicken breasts (4 oz/115 g each)	4
2	cans (14½ oz/411 g each) Italian-style chunky tomatoes	2
1	medium onion, chopped	1
	Parmesan cheese, if desired	
	Sliced ripe olives, if desired	

- Cook fettuccine according to package directions. Drain. Toss fettuccine with *1 tbsp (15 mL)* butter. Keep warm.
- Meanwhile, rub chicken breasts with Italian seasoning. In large skillet, melt remaining butter until sizzling; add chicken. Cook over medium heat, turning once, until lightly browned (7 to 10 minutes).
- In medium bowl, stir together tomatoes and onion. Add tomato mixture to chicken. Continue cooking, stirring occasionally, until mixture just comes to a boil (3 to 5 minutes). Reduce heat to low. Cover and continue cooking until chicken is no longer pink (10 to 15 minutes). Remove chicken from skillet. Keep warm.
- Increase heat to medium. Cook tomato mixture until mixture thickens slightly (6 to 8 minutes).
- To serve, spoon sauce over fettuccine. Cut chicken breast into slices; place over tomato sauce. Sprinkle with Parmesan cheese and sliced ripe olives, if desired.

4 servings

NUTRITION FACTS (1 serving)
Calories 450 • Protein 51 g • Carbohydrate 40 g
Fat 9 g • Cholesterol 115 mg • Sodium 700 mg

MUSTARD BAKED CHICKEN

***Preparation time:* 10 minutes**
***Baking time:* 50 minutes**

½ cup	sour cream (regular, light *or* fat free)	125 mL
¼ cup	country-style Dijon mustard	50 mL
1 tsp	chili purée with garlic	5 mL
3–4 lb	frying chicken, cut into 8 pieces, skin removed	1.3 to 1.8 kg

- Heat oven to 375°F (190°C). In small bowl, stir together sour cream, mustard and chili purée.
- Place chicken in 12 x 8-inch (30 x 20 cm) baking dish. Brush with sour cream mixture; *discard any remaining mixture.*
- Bake for 50 to 60 minutes or until chicken is no longer pink.

6 servings

NUTRITION FACTS (1 serving)
Calories 320 • Protein 50 g • Carbohydrate 2 g
Fat 12 g • Cholesterol 165 mg • Sodium 460 mg

CHICKEN SKILLET DINNER

***Preparation time:* 15 minutes**
***Cooking time:* 18 minutes**

¼ cup	butter	50 mL
4	boneless skinless chicken breasts (4 oz/115 g each)	4
1½ cups	uncooked quick-cooking rice	375 mL
1½ cups	water	375 mL
¼ cup	sliced green onions	50 mL
1	can (4 oz/113 g) sliced mushrooms, drained	1
1	jar (2 oz/57 g) chopped pimiento, drained	1
1 tsp	dried thyme leaves	5 mL
	Salt	
	Pepper	

- In large skillet, melt butter until sizzling; add chicken. Cook over medium heat, turning once, until chicken is no longer pink (10 to 14 minutes).
- Add all remaining ingredients. Cover and continue cooking, stirring occasionally, until rice absorbs liquid and is tender (8 to 10 minutes). Season with salt and pepper to taste.

4 servings

NUTRITION FACTS (1 serving)
Calories 440 • Protein 43 g • Carbohydrate 32 g
Fat 14 g • Cholesterol 130 mg • Sodium 360 mg

GRILLED CHICKEN WITH ORANGE SAUCE

Preparation time: 25 minutes
Grilling time: 40 minutes
Cooking time: 15 minutes

CHICKEN

3–4 lb	frying chicken, cut into 8 pieces	1.3 to 1.8 kg

SAUCE

2 tbsp	butter	30 mL
2 tbsp	finely chopped green onions	30 mL
½ tsp	finely chopped fresh garlic	2 mL
½ cup	orange juice	125 mL
1 tsp	cornstarch	5 mL
2	medium tomatoes, cubed ½-inch (1 cm)	2
1 to 2 tbsp	chopped fresh cilantro *or* parsley	15 to 30 mL
1 tsp	grated orange peel	5 mL
½ tsp	sugar	2 mL

- Heat gas grill to medium *or* charcoal grill until coals are ash white, placing coals to one side. Make aluminum foil drip pan; place opposite coals.
- Place chicken on grill over drip pan. Grill, turning once, until chicken is no longer pink (40 to 50 minutes).
- In medium saucepan, melt butter until sizzling; stir in green onions and garlic. Cook over medium heat, stirring occasionally, until onions are softened (1 to 2 minutes).
- Meanwhile, in small bowl, stir together *¼ cup (50 mL)* orange juice and cornstarch. To onion mixture, add remaining orange juice, tomatoes, cilantro, orange peel and sugar. Continue cooking until mixture comes to a full boil (4 to 5 minutes).
- Reduce heat to low. Cook, stirring occasionally, until slightly thickened (8 to 10 minutes). Serve sauce over chicken.

Broiler Directions: Heat broiler. Place chicken on greased broiler pan. Broil 6 to 8 inches (15 to 20 cm) from heat, turning every 10 minutes, until chicken is no longer pink (30 to 35 minutes). Continue as directed above.

6 servings

NUTRITION FACTS (1 serving)
Calories 390 • Protein 16 g • Carbohydrate 5 g
Fat 34 g • Cholesterol 70 mg • Sodium 95 mg

CRISPY CHICKEN IN CREAMY ONION SAUCE

Preparation time: 15 minutes
Cooking time: 1 hour 7 minutes

CHICKEN

2½–3 lb	frying chicken, cut into 8 pieces	1.1 to 1.3 kg
2 tbsp	milk	30 mL
¼ cup	cornflake crumbs	50 mL
½ tsp	salt	2 mL
½ tsp	paprika	2 mL
⅛ tsp	pepper	0.5 mL

SAUCE

1	can (10¾ oz/318 mL) condensed cream of celery *or* chicken soup	1
1 cup	light sour cream	250 mL
1	envelope (1 oz/28 g) dry onion soup mix	1
	Fresh parsley, if desired	

- Heat oven to 375°F (190°C). Place chicken, skin-side up, in 12 x 8-inch (30 x 20 cm) baking dish. Brush with milk.
- Mix cornflake crumbs and seasonings; sprinkle over chicken. Bake for 55 to 60 minutes or until chicken is crispy and no longer pink. Drain.
- Meanwhile, in small bowl, combine all sauce ingredients. Pour around, but not over, chicken pieces. Continue baking for 12 to 15 minutes or until sauce is heated through. Garnish with parsley, if desired.

4 servings

NUTRITION FACTS (1 serving)
Calories 790 • Protein 57 g • Carbohydrate 24 g
Fat 50 g • Cholesterol 280 mg • Sodium 1820 mg

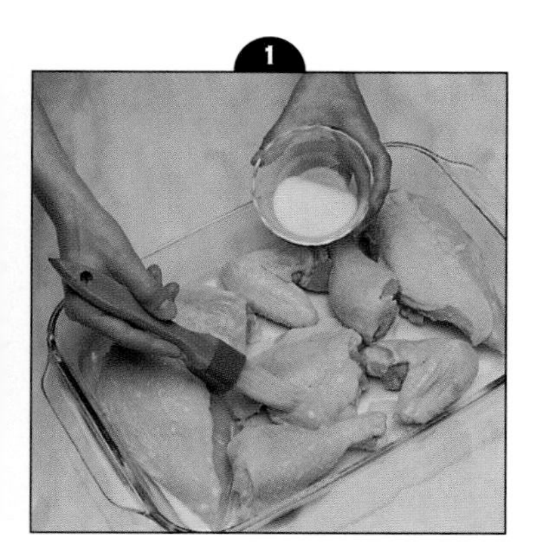

Brush chicken with milk.

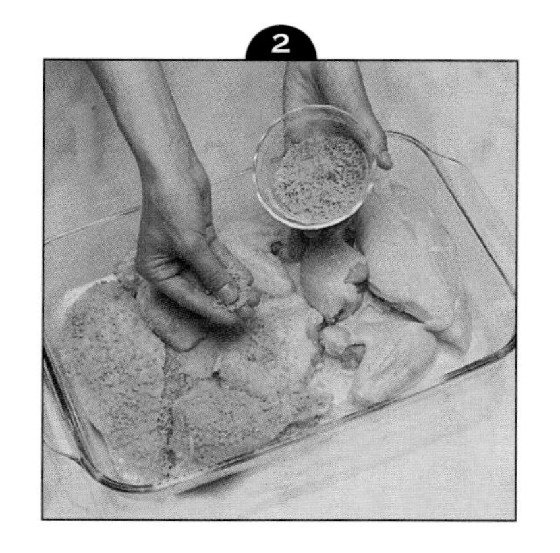

Mix cornflake crumbs and seasonings; sprinkle over chicken.

Pour sauce around, but not over, chicken pieces.

MONTEREY CHICKEN WITH BLACK BEANS AND PASTA

Preparation time: 10 minutes
Broiling time: 25 minutes
Cooking time: 3 minutes

CHICKEN

2 tbsp	olive *or* vegetable oil	30 mL
1 tsp	Italian seasoning*	5 mL
½ tsp	salt	2 mL
½ tsp	pepper	2 mL
4	split chicken breasts	4

PASTA

6 oz	uncooked dried linguine	170 g

BEANS

½ cup	sliced green onions	125 mL
1	can (15 oz/425 g) black beans, rinsed, drained	1
1	can (14½ oz/411 g) Italian *or* Mexican-style stewed tomatoes	1
1 tbsp	chopped seeded jalapeño pepper *or* green chilies	15 mL
1 cup	shredded Monterey Jack cheese	250 mL
	Fresh oregano leaves, if desired	

- Heat broiler. In small bowl, stir together oil, Italian seasoning, salt and pepper.
- Place chicken breasts on broiler pan; brush with *half* of oil mixture. Broil 4 to 6 inches (10 to 15 cm) from heat, turning once and basting with remaining oil mixture, until chicken is no longer pink (25 to 30 minutes).
- Meanwhile, cook linguine according to package directions. Drain and keep warm.
- In medium saucepan, combine all beans ingredients *except* cheese. Cook over medium-low heat, stirring occasionally, until heated through (3 to 4 minutes).
- Serve chicken and bean mixture over hot cooked linguine; sprinkle with cheese. Garnish with oregano, if desired.

** Substitute ¼ tsp (1 mL) each dried oregano, marjoram and basil leaves, and ⅛ tsp (0.5 mL) rubbed sage.*

4 servings

NUTRITION FACTS (1 serving)
Calories 610 • Protein 40 g • Carbohydrate 54 g
Fat 26 g • Cholesterol 90 mg • Sodium 1030 mg

San Diego Couscous Dinner

Preparation time: 10 minutes
Cooking time: 12 minutes

2 tsp	**vegetable oil**	**10 mL**
¾–1 lb	**boneless skinless chicken breasts, seasoned as desired (salt, pepper, chili powder, garlic salt, etc.)**	**350 to 450 g**
1	**medium zucchini, thinly sliced**	**1**
2 cups	**hot cooked couscous***	**500 mL**
1 cup	**thick and chunky salsa, heated**	**250 mL**
¾ cup	**shredded taco-flavored light cheese**	**175 mL**
¾ cup	**light *or* fat free sour cream**	**175 mL**

- In large nonstick skillet, heat oil; add chicken. Cook over medium-high heat, turning occasionally, until chicken is no longer pink (10 to 12 minutes). Remove chicken from skillet. Cut chicken into ½-inch (1 cm) strips and keep warm.
- In same skillet, place zucchini. Cook over medium heat, stirring occasionally, until crisply tender (2 to 3 minutes).
- To serve, spoon hot couscous onto large serving platter. Spoon ½ *cup (125 mL)* salsa over couscous. Top with chicken and zucchini; sprinkle with cheese. Spoon remaining salsa over chicken and zucchini; dollop with sour cream.

* *Substitute 2 cups (500 mL) hot cooked rice.*

4 servings

NUTRITION FACTS (1 serving)
Calories 350 • Protein 30 g • Carbohydrate 31 g
Fat 11 g • Cholesterol 70 mg • Sodium 320 mg

ITALIAN-STYLE CHICKEN AND POTATOES

Preparation time: 15 minutes
Baking time: 1 hour 13 minutes

¼ cup	**butter**	**50 mL**
1½ cups	**water**	**375 mL**
1	**can (16 oz/454 g) Italian-flavored stewed tomatoes**	**1**
1	**package (5 oz/142 g) dried scalloped potatoes**	**1**
1 tsp	**dried Italian seasoning**	**5 mL**
6	**split chicken breasts, skinned**	**6**
1 cup	**shredded Cheddar cheese**	**250 mL**

- Heat oven to 350°F (180°C). In 13 x 9-inch (33 x 23 cm) baking pan, melt butter in oven (5 to 7 minutes).
- Meanwhile, in medium saucepan, stir together water, tomatoes, scalloped potato mix and Italian seasoning.
- Cook over medium heat, stirring occasionally, until mixture comes to a full boil (10 to 12 minutes). Boil, stirring occasionally, 3 minutes. Spoon into prepared baking pan.
- Dip chicken pieces into melted butter; place chicken over potato mixture.
- Cover with aluminum foil; bake for 15 minutes. Remove foil and continue baking for 45 to 50 minutes. Sprinkle cheese over chicken. Continue baking for 8 to 10 minutes or until cheese is melted and chicken is no longer pink.

6 servings

NUTRITION FACTS (1 serving)
Calories 470 • Protein 32 g • Carbohydrate 22 g
Fat 29 g • Cholesterol 110 mg • Sodium 1430 mg

Chicken 'n Cheese Pizzas

Preparation time: 20 minutes
Baking time: 12 minutes

¼ cup	pesto	50 mL
4	6-inch (15 cm) round pre-baked Italian bread shells *or* focaccia	4
1½ cups	chopped cooked chicken	375 mL
⅓ cup	chopped red *or* white onion	75 mL
¼ cup	sliced pitted ripe olives	50 mL
1	large tomato, cubed ½-inch (1 cm)	1
1 cup	shredded mozzarella cheese	250 mL

- Heat oven to 425°F (220°C). Spread *1 tbsp (15 mL)* pesto on each bread shell. Place on baking sheet.
- Arrange chicken, onion, olives and tomato on bread shells; top with cheese.
- Bake for 12 to 15 minutes or until heated through.

4 servings

NUTRITION FACTS (1 serving)
Calories 610 • Protein 39 g • Carbohydrate 55 g
Fat 25 g • Cholesterol 75 mg • Sodium 1070 mg

Orange Honey Broiled Chicken

Preparation time: 10 minutes
Broiling time: 25 minutes

3–3½ lb	frying chicken, cut into 8 pieces	1.3 to 1.6 kg
½ cup	Honey Butter	125 mL
¼ cup	frozen orange juice concentrate, thawed	50 mL
1 tsp	paprika	5 mL
	Salt	
	Pepper	

- Heat broiler. Place chicken pieces on aluminum foil-lined broiler pan.
- In small saucepan, melt honey butter; stir in orange juice concentrate and paprika.
- Broil chicken 6 to 8 inches (15 to 20 cm) from heat, basting with orange juice mixture, for 15 to 20 minutes. Turn and continue broiling until chicken is no longer pink (10 to 15 minutes). Season with salt and pepper.

4 servings

NUTRITION FACTS (1 serving)
Calories 280 • Protein 35 g • Carbohydrate 4 g
Fat 13 g • Cholesterol 115 mg • Sodium 120 mg

Meat

ITALIAN-STYLE PORK CUTLETS

Preparation time: 5 minutes
Cooking time: 16 minutes

CUTLETS

1 tbsp	Roasted Garlic Butter with Olive Oil *or* butter	15 mL
1 lb	boneless pork loin, cut into 8 slices, about ¼-inch (5 mm) thick	450 g
¼ tsp	coarsely ground pepper	1 mL

SAUCE

1 tsp	finely chopped fresh garlic	5 mL
½ tsp	dried rosemary, crushed	2 mL
½ cup	chicken broth	125 mL
1	can (2¼ oz/64 g) sliced ripe olives, drained	1
1	medium tomato, cut into 12 wedges	1

- In large skillet, melt garlic butter until sizzling; add pork slices and pepper. Cook over medium-high heat, turning occasionally, until pork is no longer pink (8 to 12 minutes). Remove pork from skillet and keep warm.
- To same skillet, add garlic and rosemary. Continue cooking until garlic begins to brown (2 to 3 minutes).
- Stir in chicken broth. Continue cooking, stirring constantly, until mixture comes to a full boil and thickens (5 to 8 minutes).
- Stir in olives and tomato. Continue cooking until heated through (1 minute). Serve sauce over meat.

4 servings

NUTRITION FACTS (1 serving)
Calories 210 • Protein 26 g • Carbohydrate 3 g
Fat 10 g • Cholesterol 75 mg • Sodium 340 mg

VEAL MARSALA WITH MUSHROOMS

Preparation time: 15 minutes
Cooking time: 8 minutes

½ cup	**vegetable broth**	**125 mL**
10	**sun-dried tomatoes**	**10**
¾ lb	**veal sirloin, cut into 4 pieces**	**350 g**
¼ cup	**chopped green onions**	**50 mL**
1 tbsp	**chopped fresh basil leaves***	**15 mL**
1 tsp	**finely chopped fresh garlic**	**5 mL**
½ tsp	**salt**	**2 mL**
¼ tsp	**coarsely ground pepper**	**1 mL**
¼ cup	**dry Marsala wine *or* apple juice**	**50 mL**
8 oz	**mushrooms (shiitake, button *and/or* crimini), sliced**	**225 g**
2 cups	**hot cooked pasta**	**500 mL**

- In small bowl, stir together vegetable broth and tomatoes; set aside.
- Place veal between two pieces of plastic food wrap. Pound with meat mallet or rolling pin to ¼-inch (5 mm) thickness.
- Spray large skillet with no stick cooking spray. Add tomato mixture, *2 tbsp (30 mL)* green onions, basil, garlic, salt and pepper. Cook over medium-high heat, stirring occasionally, until mixture comes to a full boil (2 to 3 minutes).
- Add veal. Continue cooking, turning once, until lightly browned (2 to 3 minutes). Add wine and mushrooms. Continue cooking, stirring occasionally, until veal and mushrooms are tender (4 to 5 minutes).
- Serve over hot cooked pasta.

** Substitute 1 tsp (5 mL) dried basil leaves.*

4 servings

NUTRITION FACTS (1 serving)
Calories 280 • Protein 26 g • Carbohydrate 27 g
Fat 7 g • Cholesterol 75 mg • Sodium 590 mg

SPICY BEEF AND TOMATOES WITH FETTUCCINE

Preparation time: 25 minutes
Cooking time: 9 minutes

4 oz	uncooked dried fettuccine	115 g
2 tbsp	butter	30 mL
2	serrano peppers, seeded, chopped	2
1	medium onion, sliced into rings, separated	1
2 tbsp	chopped fresh basil leaves*	30 mL
1 tsp	finely chopped fresh garlic	5 mL
¾ lb	beef sirloin, cut into thin strips	350 g
8	Roma tomatoes, cut into eighths	8
½ tsp	salt	2 mL
¼ tsp	pepper	1 mL
⅓ cup	freshly grated Romano *or* Parmesan cheese	75 mL

- Cook fettuccine according to package directions. Drain and keep warm.
- Meanwhile, in large skillet, melt butter until sizzling; add peppers, onion, basil and garlic. Cook over medium-high heat, stirring constantly, until onion is softened (2 to 3 minutes).
- Stir in beef strips. Continue cooking, stirring occasionally, until beef is lightly browned (4 to 6 minutes). Add all remaining ingredients *except* cheese. Continue cooking until tomatoes are heated through (3 to 6 minutes).
- To serve, spoon beef mixture over cooked fettuccine; sprinkle with cheese.

** Substitute 2 tsp (10 mL) dried basil leaves.*

4 servings

NUTRITION FACTS (1 serving)
Calories 350 • Protein 26 g • Carbohydrate 32 g
Fat 13 g • Cholesterol 75 mg • Sodium 490 mg

GREEN CHILI BURGERS

Preparation time: 10 minutes
Grilling time: 10 minutes

BURGERS

¼ cup	finely chopped onion	50 mL
1 lb	lean ground beef	450 g
1	can (4 oz/113 g) chopped green chilies	1
1 tsp	hot pepper sauce	5 mL
½ tsp	salt	2 mL
4	whole wheat hamburger buns	4
4	slices Jalapeño Jack pasteurized process cheese	4

TOPPINGS

- Jalapeño peppers
- Lettuce
- Salsa
- Tomato slices

- Heat gas grill to medium *or* charcoal grill until coals are ash white.
- Meanwhile, in medium bowl, combine onion, ground beef, chilies, hot pepper sauce and salt; mix lightly. Shape into four ¾-inch (2 cm) thick patties.
- Place patties on grill. Grill, turning once, until cooked as desired (10 to 12 minutes).
- To serve, place burgers on buns; top with cheese slices. Serve with desired toppings.

4 sandwiches

NUTRITION FACTS
(1 sandwich without toppings)
Calories 520 • Protein 29 g • Carbohydrate 26 g
Fat 33 g • Cholesterol 105 mg • Sodium 1040 mg

TEX MEX CASSEROLE

Preparation time: 20 minutes
Cooking time: 30 minutes

1 lb	ground beef	450 g
¼ cup	chopped onion	50 mL
1	can (15 oz/425 g) black beans, rinsed, drained	1
1	can (8 oz/237 mL) tomato sauce	1
1	package (1.25 oz/35 g) taco seasoning mix	1
8 oz	American cheese, cubed ½-inch (1 cm)	225 g
1	package (8½ oz/241 g) corn muffin mix	1
	Milk	
	Egg	

- Heat oven to 350°F (180°C). In large skillet, cook ground beef and onion over medium heat, stirring occasionally, until browned (4 to 5 minutes). Drain off fat.
- Stir in beans, tomato sauce and seasoning mix. Continue cooking until heated through (3 to 4 minutes). Stir in cheese.
- Prepare corn muffin mix according to package directions using milk and egg; set aside.
- In medium casserole, spoon in beef mixture; top with muffin batter. Bake for 30 to 35 minutes or until heated through and cheese is melted.

6 servings

NUTRITION FACTS (1 serving)
Calories 550 • Protein 31 g • Carbohydrate 45 g
Fat 27 g • Cholesterol 135 mg • Sodium 1520 mg

FIESTA STEAK

Preparation time: 15 minutes
Marinating time: 4 hours
Cooking time: 10 minutes

MARINADE

1 cup	salsa	250 mL
2 tsp	ground cumin	10 mL
1 tsp	grated lime peel	5 mL
2 tsp	lime juice	10 mL

STEAK

1 lb	top round beef steak, ½-inch (1 cm) thick	450 g

- In large resealable plastic food bag, combine all marinade ingredients; add steak. Tightly seal bag. Turn to coat steak well. Place in 13 x 9-inch (33 x 23 cm) pan. Refrigerate at least 4 hours or overnight.
- Heat gas grill to medium *or* charcoal grill until coals are ash white. Remove steak from marinade; *reserve marinade.*
- Place steak on grill. Grill, turning occasionally, until cooked as desired (10 to 12 minutes).
- Meanwhile, in small saucepan, bring reserved marinade to a full boil. To serve, slice steak across grain; serve with hot marinade.

4 servings

NUTRITION FACTS (1 serving)
Calories 170 • Protein 25 g • Carbohydrate 8 g
Fat 4 g • Cholesterol 65 mg • Sodium 440 mg

PORK CHOPS WITH CARAMELIZED ONIONS

Preparation time: 5 minutes
Cooking time: 20 minutes

2 tbsp	Roasted Garlic Butter with Olive Oil	30 mL
4	pork chops, ½-inch (1 cm) thick	4
½ tsp	salt	2 mL
½ tsp	coarsely ground pepper	2 mL
3	medium onions, thinly sliced	3
½ tsp	dried thyme leaves*	2 mL

- In large skillet, melt garlic butter until sizzling; add pork chops. Cook over medium-high heat, turning once, until browned (8 to 10 minutes). Season with salt and pepper. Remove chops to serving platter and keep warm.
- Place onions in pan with pan juices; sprinkle with thyme. Continue cooking, stirring occasionally, until onions are caramelized (8 to 10 minutes).
- Return chops to pan; continue cooking until pork is no longer pink (4 to 5 minutes).

* *Substitute ¼ tsp (1 mL) dried rosemary.*

4 servings

NUTRITION FACTS (1 serving)
Calories 220 • Protein 23 g • Carbohydrate 8 g
Fat 11 g • Cholesterol 70 mg • Sodium 390 mg

HAM 'N VEGGIE PASTA DINNER

Preparation time: 15 minutes
Cooking time: 7 minutes

8 oz	uncooked dried fettuccine *or* rigatoni	225 g
3 tbsp	butter	45 mL
2 cups	fresh broccoli florets	500 mL
¼ cup	chopped onion	50 mL
1	small red pepper, cut into strips	1
¾ cup	milk	175 mL
3 tbsp	all-purpose flour	45 mL
1 cup	shredded Monterey Jack *or* mozzarella cheese	250 mL
½ cup	sour cream (regular, light *or* fat free)	125 mL
4 oz	ham, cut into strips	115 g
¼ tsp	salt	1 mL
¼ tsp	pepper	1 mL
¼ tsp	ground sage	1 mL

- Cook fettuccine according to package directions. Drain.
- Meanwhile, in large skillet, melt butter until sizzling; add broccoli, onion and red pepper. Cook over medium heat, stirring occasionally, until broccoli is crisply tender (3 to 4 minutes).
- In small bowl, stir together milk and flour. Add to broccoli mixture; stir in all remaining ingredients. Continue cooking, stirring constantly, until mixture thickens (2 to 3 minutes).
- Add cooked fettuccine; continue cooking, stirring constantly, until heated through (2 to 3 minutes). Serve immediately.

6 servings

NUTRITION FACTS (1 serving)
Calories 380 • Protein 15 g • Carbohydrate 37 g
Fat 19 g • Cholesterol 60 mg • Sodium 540 mg

Hungarian Meatballs Imperial

Preparation time: 20 minutes
Cooking time: 38 minutes

MEATBALLS

½ cup	dry bread crumbs	125 mL
⅓ cup	milk	75 mL
1½ lbs	ground beef	675 g
1	egg	1
1 tsp	prepared mustard	5 mL
½ tsp	garlic salt	2 mL
⅛ tsp	pepper	0.5 mL
2 tbsp	oil	30 mL

SAUCE

1 cup	onion slices, ⅛-inch (3 mm), separated into rings	250 mL
1	can (15 oz/444 mL) tomato sauce	1
1	can (4 oz/113 g) mushroom stems and pieces, drained	1
1 tbsp	paprika	15 mL
2 tsp	instant beef bouillon	10 mL
½ cup	water	125 mL
3 tbsp	all-purpose flour	45 mL
1 cup	sour cream (regular, light *or* fat free)	250 ml
	Hot cooked rice *or* noodles	

- In large bowl, combine all meatball ingredients *except* oil; mix well. Shape into 16 meatballs.
- In large skillet, heat oil; add meatballs. Cook over medium heat, turning occasionally, until meatballs are browned on all sides (8 to 10 minutes).
- Reduce heat to low. Add onion, tomato sauce, mushrooms, paprika and bouillon. Cover and cook until meatballs are heated through (20 to 25 minutes).
- Meanwhile, combine water and flour; add to meat sauce mixture. Continue cooking, stirring occasionally, 5 minutes. Add sour cream; continue cooking, stirring until smooth and heated through (5 to 6 minutes). Serve over hot cooked rice.

8 servings

NUTRITION FACTS (1 serving)
Calories 320 • Protein 20 g • Carbohydrate 16 g
Fat 20 g • Cholesterol 95 mg • Sodium 770 mg

1

In large bowl, combine all meatball ingredients except oil; mix well.

2

Shape into 16 meatballs.

3

Cook meatballs over medium heat, turning occasionally, until browned on all sides.

Add onion, tomato sauce, mushrooms, paprika and bouillon. Cover and cook until meatballs are heated through.

Combine water and flour; add to meat sauce mixture. Continue cooking, stirring occasionally, 5 minutes.

Add sour cream; continue cooking, stirring until smooth and heated through.

CHEESEBURGER VEGETABLE MEAT LOAF

Preparation time: 10 minutes
Baking time: 1 hour 3 minutes

2 cups	frozen vegetable combination (broccoli, onion and red pepper), thawed*	500 mL
1 cup	Italian dry bread crumbs	250 mL
¼ cup	ketchup	50 mL
1½ lbs	ground beef**	675 g
1	egg	1
1 tbsp	prepared mustard	15 mL
1 tsp	onion salt	5 mL
¼ tsp	pepper	1 mL
3	slices American cheese, cut in half diagonally	3

- Heat oven to 350°F (180°C). In large bowl, mix together all ingredients *except* cheese slices. Place mixture in 9 x 5-inch (23 x 13 cm) loaf pan. Bake for 60 to 75 minutes or until beef is cooked through.
- Place cheese triangles on top. Continue baking for 3 to 5 minutes or until cheese is melted. Let stand in pan 10 minutes. Loosen sides and carefully remove from pan.

** Substitute 2 cups (500 mL) of your favorite frozen or fresh vegetable combination.*

*** Substitute 1½ lbs (675 g) purchased meat loaf mixture (beef, pork and veal).*

6 servings

NUTRITION FACTS (1 serving)
Calories 460 • Protein 27 g • Carbohydrate 24 g
Fat 28 g • Cholesterol 125 mg • Sodium 840 mg

PORK AND CABBAGE CASSEROLE

Preparation time: 25 minutes
Baking time: 40 minutes

4	boneless center-cut pork loin chops, about ½-inch (1 cm) thick	4
¾ tsp	salt	3 mL
¼ tsp	pepper	1 mL
2 cups	shredded refrigerated potatoes	500 mL
2	medium onions, chopped	2
4 cups	coleslaw mix	1 L
1 tbsp	caraway seeds, if desired	15 mL
½ cup	apple juice	125 mL

- Heat oven to 350°F (180°C). Lightly spray large skillet with no stick cooking spray. Add pork chops, *¼ tsp (1 mL)* salt and pepper. Cook over medium-high heat, turning occasionally, until lightly browned (6 to 8 minutes).
- Meanwhile, in large casserole, stir together remaining salt and all remaining ingredients *except* apple juice. Top casserole with browned pork chops.
- Reduce heat under skillet to medium; add apple juice. Cook, stirring and scraping pan constantly, until heated through (1 to 2 minutes). Pour juice over chops. Cover and bake for 40 to 50 minutes or until pork is no longer pink.

4 servings

NUTRITION FACTS (1 serving)
Calories 340 • Protein 31 g • Carbohydrate 34 g
Fat 10 g • Cholesterol 75 mg • Sodium 600 mg

BARBECUED HAM AND PEACHES

***Preparation time:** 10 minutes*
***Baking time:** 36 minutes*

1	ham slice, about 1 lb (450 g)	1
½ cup	sugar	125 mL
½ cup	chili sauce	125 mL
1 tbsp	lemon juice	15 mL
2 tsp	Worcestershire sauce	10 mL
½ tsp	chili powder	2 mL
1	can (16 oz/454 g) peach halves, drained	1

- Heat oven to 325°F (160°C). In 12 x 8-inch (30 x 20 cm) baking dish, place ham slice. Bake for 18 to 20 minutes or until heated through.
- Meanwhile, in small saucepan, combine sugar, chili sauce, lemon juice, Worcestershire sauce and chili powder. Cook over medium heat, stirring occasionally, until mixture just comes to a boil. Remove from heat; add peaches. Gently stir to coat peaches.
- Spoon peaches over ham in baking dish; pour sauce over ham. Continue baking, basting occasionally, for 18 to 20 minutes or until heated through.

4 servings

NUTRITION FACTS (1 serving)
Calories 510 • Protein 30 g • Carbohydrate 48 g
Fat 23 g • Cholesterol 105 mg • Sodium 550 mg

MUSTARD 'N ONION GLAZED PORK CHOPS

***Preparation time:** 10 minutes*
***Broiling time:** 14 minutes*

¼ cup	Dijon-style mustard	50 mL
1	medium onion, cut into 2-inch (5 cm) strips	1
1 tbsp	firmly packed brown sugar	15 mL
2 tbsp	orange marmalade	30 mL
4	center-cut pork chops, ½-inch (1 cm) thick	4

- In small bowl, stir together mustard, onion, brown sugar and marmalade; set aside.
- *Heat broiler.* Spray broiler pan with no stick cooking spray. Place chops on broiler pan; spread each with *1 tbsp (15 mL)* mustard mixture. Broil 4 to 6 inches (10 to 15 cm) from heat, turning once and spreading with remaining mustard mixture, until pork is no longer pink (14 to 16 minutes).

4 servings

NUTRITION FACTS (1 serving)
Calories 310 • Protein 26 g • Carbohydrate 14 g
Fat 17 g • Cholesterol 85 mg • Sodium 460 mg

TOMATO BEEF STROGANOFF

***Preparation time:* 10 minutes**
***Cooking time:* 10 minutes**

8 oz	**uncooked medium egg noodles**	**225 g**
1 lb	**pre-cut beef stir-fry meat**	**450 g**
8 oz	**sliced mushrooms**	**225 g**
¼ cup	**all-purpose flour**	**50 mL**
1	**can (14½ oz/429 mL) beef broth**	**1**
1	**can (14½ oz/411 g) stewed tomatoes**	**1**
1 cup	**sour cream (regular, light *or* fat free)**	**250 mL**
	Freshly ground pepper	

- Cook noodles according to package directions. Drain and keep warm.
- Meanwhile, spray large deep skillet with no stick cooking spray; add beef. Cook over medium heat, stirring occasionally, until browned (4 to 5 minutes). Drain. Add mushrooms. Continue cooking, stirring constantly, 2 minutes.
- In small bowl, stir together flour and broth. Add broth mixture and tomatoes to beef. Continue cooking, stirring constantly, until mixture boils (1 to 2 minutes). Continue boiling, stirring constantly, 1 minute. Remove from heat; stir in sour cream.
- Serve sauce over hot cooked noodles. Season to taste with freshly ground pepper.

4 servings

NUTRITION FACTS (1 serving)
Calories 580 • Protein 30 g • Carbohydrate 59 g
Fat 21 g • Cholesterol 155 mg • Sodium 740 mg

Garlic Pepper Steak with Root Vegetables

Preparation time: 15 minutes
Cooking time: 16 minutes

¼ cup	butter	50 mL
1 tbsp	finely chopped fresh garlic	15 mL
1 tsp	coarsely ground pepper	5 mL
½ tsp	salt	2 mL
4	medium carrots, sliced ¼-inch (5 mm)	4
1	medium leek, sliced ¼-inch (5 mm)	1
1	medium turnip, cut into thin wedges	1
1 lb	beef sirloin steak, cut into 4 pieces*	450 g

- In large skillet, melt 2 *tbsp (30 mL)* butter until sizzling; stir in garlic, pepper and salt. Add carrots, leek and turnip. Cook over medium-high heat, stirring occasionally, until vegetables are crisply tender and caramelized (8 to 10 minutes).
- Remove vegetables from pan. Add remaining butter and beef sirloin. Cook meat, turning once, 6 minutes. Add vegetables; continue cooking until meat is cooked as desired (2 to 4 minutes).

** Substitute 1 lb (450 g) beef eye of round steaks.*

4 servings

NUTRITION FACTS (1 serving)
Calories 310 • Protein 24 g • Carbohydrate 15 g
Fat 17 g • Cholesterol 100 mg • Sodium 480 mg

THREE-CHEESE BEEF ENCHILADAS

Preparation time: 30 minutes
Baking time: 32 minutes

½ cup	vegetable oil	125 mL
8	8-inch (20 cm) flour tortillas*	8
1½ cups	sour cream (regular, light *or* fat free)	375 mL
4 oz	cream cheese, softened	115 g
2½ cups	shredded cooked beef	625 mL
1 cup	shredded Cheddar cheese	250 mL
2 cups	shredded Monterey Jack cheese	500 mL
¼ cup	chopped green onions	50 mL
½ tsp	salt	2 mL
½ tsp	ground cumin	2 mL
1	can (10 oz/296 mL) enchilada sauce	1

- Heat oven to 350°F (180°C). In large skillet, heat oil over medium heat, 2 to 3 minutes. With tongs, dip each tortilla in hot oil, coating lightly; set aside.
- In large bowl, stir together sour cream and cream cheese until smooth. Stir in beef, Cheddar cheese, *1 cup (250 mL)* Monterey Jack cheese, green onions, salt and cumin. Place *½ cup (125 mL)* beef mixture in center of each tortilla; roll up tortillas. Place in 12 x 8-inch (30 x 20 cm) baking dish, seam-side down. Bake for 15 minutes.
- Pour enchilada sauce over tortillas; spread to cover. Continue baking for 12 to 15 minutes or until heated through. Sprinkle with remaining Monterey Jack cheese. Continue baking for 1 to 2 minutes or until cheese is melted.

** Substitute eight 6-inch (15 cm) corn tortillas.*

8 servings

NUTRITION FACTS (1 serving)
Calories 670 • Protein 30 g • Carbohydrate 26 g
Fat 50 g • Cholesterol 140 mg • Sodium 690 mg

With tongs, dip each tortilla in hot oil, coating lightly.

Stir beef, Cheddar cheese and 1 cup (250 mL) Monterey Jack cheese into sour cream mixture.

Place ½ cup (125 mL) beef mixture in center of each tortilla.

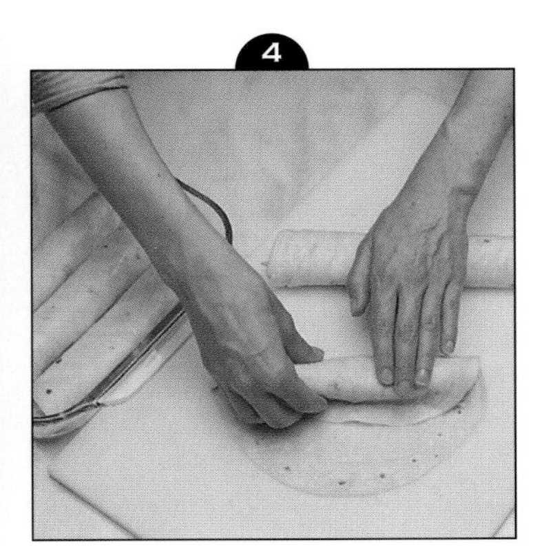

Roll up tortillas. Place in baking dish, seam-side down.

Pour enchilada sauce over tortillas; spread to cover.

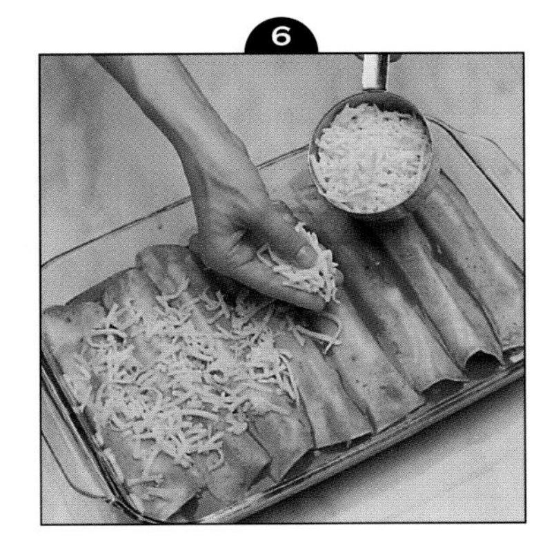

Sprinkle with remaining Monterey Jack cheese.

Fish and Seafood

SALMON STEAKS WITH LIME SAUCE

Preparation time: 15 minutes
Grilling time: 12 minutes

LIME SAUCE

3 tbsp	**butter, melted**	**45 mL**
1 tbsp	**chopped fresh marjoram leaves***	**15 mL**
1 tsp	**lime juice**	**5 mL**
⅛ tsp	**pepper**	**0.5 mL**

SALMON

4	**salmon steaks, 6 oz (170 g) each**	**4**
4	**thin slices lime**	**4**

- Prepare grill, placing coals to one side; heat until coals are ash white. Make aluminum foil drip pan; place opposite coals.
- In small bowl, stir together all lime sauce ingredients. Brush both sides of salmon steaks with lime sauce.
- Place salmon steaks on grill over drip pan. Cover and grill 6 minutes. Turn fish; brush with lime sauce. Top each salmon steak with *1 slice* lime. Cover and continue grilling until fish flakes with a fork (6 to 8 minutes).

** Substitute 1 tsp (5 mL) dried marjoram leaves.*

4 servings

NUTRITION FACTS (1 serving)
Calories 230 • Protein 29 g • Carbohydrate 1 g
Fat 11 g • Cholesterol 85 mg • Sodium 85 mg

SHRIMP PRIMAVERA SUPPER

Preparation time: 20 minutes
Cooking time: 24 minutes

1½ cups	uncooked dried medium pasta shells	375 mL
⅓ cup	butter	75 mL
1	package (12 oz/340 g) frozen raw cocktail-size shrimp, thawed, deveined, rinsed	1
¼ cup	all-purpose flour	50 mL
2 cups	milk	500 mL
2 tbsp	chopped fresh parsley	30 mL
1 tsp	dried marjoram leaves	5 mL
1 tsp	garlic salt	5 mL
1	bay leaf	1
¼ tsp	hot pepper sauce	1 mL
1	bag (16 oz/454 g) frozen broccoli, carrots, water chestnuts and red peppers, thawed, well drained	1

- Cook pasta according to package directions. Drain. Set aside.
- In large deep skillet, melt butter until sizzling; add shrimp. Cook over medium heat, stirring occasionally, until shrimp turn pink (5 to 7 minutes). Remove shrimp; set aside.
- In same skillet, stir flour into remaining butter. Cook over medium heat 1 minute. With wire whisk, stir in milk, parsley, marjoram, garlic salt, bay leaf and hot pepper sauce. Cook over medium heat, stirring often, until sauce is thickened and comes to a full boil (6 to 8 minutes); boil 1 minute. Remove bay leaf.
- Stir in cooked pasta, vegetables and shrimp. Continue cooking, stirring occasionally, until mixture is heated through (5 to 7 minutes).

4 servings

NUTRITION FACTS (1 serving)
Calories 490 • Protein 29 g • Carbohydrate 48 g
Fat 20 g • Cholesterol 180 mg • Sodium 630 mg

1

In large deep skillet, melt butter until sizzling; add shrimp.

2

In same skillet, stir flour into remaining butter.

3

With whisk, stir in milk, parsley, marjoram, garlic salt, bay leaf and hot pepper sauce.

4

Stir in cooked pasta, vegetables and shrimp.

CRUNCHY FISH AND SPUDS

Preparation time: 30 minutes
Baking time: 45 minutes

¼ cup	**butter**	**50 mL**
2	**medium potatoes, sliced ¼-inch (5 mm)**	**2**
¾ cup	**crushed cornflakes**	**175 mL**
1 tbsp	**chopped fresh parsley**	**15 mL**
1 tsp	**paprika**	**5 mL**
¾ tsp	**garlic salt**	**3 mL**
1 lb	**walleye, red snapper *or* orange roughy fillets**	**450 g**

- Heat oven to 350°F (180°C). In 13 x 9-inch (33 x 23 cm) baking pan, melt butter in oven (5 to 7 minutes).
- Add potato slices to prepared pan; stir to coat. Cover with aluminum foil. Bake for 20 to 25 minutes or until potato slices are fork tender.
- Meanwhile, in 9-inch (23 cm) pie pan, stir together all remaining ingredients *except* walleye fillets.
- Spoon potatoes to one side of baking pan. Dip fish into melted butter in pan, then coat with cornflake mixture. Place fish opposite potatoes in same pan.
- Sprinkle fish and potatoes with remaining cornflake mixture. Bake for 20 to 30 minutes or until fish flakes with a fork.

4 servings

NUTRITION FACTS (1 serving)
Calories 280 • Protein 22 g • Carbohydrate 19 g
Fat 12 g • Cholesterol 80 mg • Sodium 530 mg

RATATOUILLE HALIBUT

Preparation time: 20 minutes
Cooking time: 19 minutes

2 cups	cubed peeled eggplant, 1-inch (2.5 cm)	500 mL
1	can (14½ oz/429 mL) Italian-style diced tomatoes	1
1	small zucchini, sliced	1
1 lb	fresh *or* frozen halibut steaks, 1-inch (2.5 cm) thick, thawed	450 g
	Salt	
	Pepper	

- In large skillet, combine all ingredients *except* fish. Bring to full boil over high heat (4 to 5 minutes).
- Reduce heat to medium. Cook until vegetables are tender (7 to 9 minutes).
- Place fish in single layer on top of vegetables. Reduce heat to medium-low. Cover and cook until fish flakes with a fork (8 to 10 minutes). Season to taste with salt and pepper.

4 servings

NUTRITION FACTS (1 serving)
Calories 170 • Protein 25 g • Carbohydrate 11 g
Fat 3 g • Cholesterol 35 mg • Sodium 320 mg

ITALIAN BUTTER CRUMB PERCH

***Preparation time:* 15 minutes**
***Baking time:* 25 minutes**

½ cup	fine dry bread crumbs	125 mL
1	package (0.7 oz/20 g) Italian salad dressing mix	1
1 tsp	dried oregano leaves	5 mL
1 tsp	dried rosemary	5 mL
¼ tsp	paprika	1 mL
1 lb	fresh perch fillets	450 g
⅓ cup	butter, melted	75 mL

- Heat oven to 350°F (180°C). In 9-inch (23 cm) pie pan, combine all ingredients *except* fillets and butter; mix well. Dip fillets in melted butter, then roll in crumb mixture to coat.
- Place in 13 x 9-inch (33 x 23 cm) baking pan. Sprinkle with remaining crumb mixture; drizzle with remaining butter. Bake for 25 to 30 minutes or until fish flakes with fork.

4 servings

NUTRITION FACTS (1 serving)
Calories 300 • Protein 23 g • Carbohydrate 12 g
Fat 18 g • Cholesterol 90 mg • Sodium 380 mg

GRILLED ITALIAN SOLE

***Preparation time:* 25 minutes**
***Grilling time:* 10 minutes**

1 lb	fresh *or* frozen sole fillets, thawed, drained	450 g
8	slices Monterey Jack cheese	8
¼ cup	sliced pitted ripe olives	50 mL
2	medium zucchini, cut into julienne strips	2
½	small onion, cut into rings	½
½	medium red pepper, thinly sliced	½
½ tsp	Italian seasoning*	2 mL
½ tsp	garlic salt	2 mL

- Heat gas grill to medium *or* charcoal grill until coals are ash white.
- Place each fish fillet in center of 18-inch (46 cm) square piece of heavy-duty aluminum foil. Top each fillet with 2 slices of cheese, olives, zucchini, onion and red pepper; sprinkle with Italian seasoning and garlic salt. Bring edges of foil up to center; tightly seal top and sides.
- Place foil packets on grill. Grill until fish flakes with a fork (10 to 14 minutes).

** Substitute ⅛ tsp (0.5 mL) each oregano, marjoram and basil leaves, with a dash of rubbed sage.*

4 servings

NUTRITION FACTS (1 serving)
Calories 240 • Protein 29 g • Carbohydrate 5 g
Fat 11 g • Cholesterol 85 mg • Sodium 420 mg

BAKED FISH WITH FENNEL

Preparation time: 20 minutes
Baking time: 30 minutes

1½ lbs	**orange roughy, walleye *or* cod fillets**	**675 g**
1 lb	**fresh asparagus spears, trimmed**	**450 g**
1	**bulb fresh fennel, sliced ¼-inch (5 mm), separated into pieces**	**1**
2 tbsp	**chopped fresh fennel weed**	**30 mL**
1 tbsp	**grated orange peel**	**15 mL**
2 tbsp	**butter**	**30 mL**
2 tbsp	**orange juice**	**30 mL**
½ tsp	**salt**	**2 mL**
½ tsp	**coarsely ground pepper**	**2 mL**
½ tsp	**finely chopped fresh garlic**	**2 mL**

- Heat oven to 350°F (180°C). In 13 x 9-inch (33 x 23 cm) baking pan, place fish fillets, skin-side down. Place asparagus and fennel pieces on top and around fish.
- In small bowl, stir together all remaining ingredients; pour over fish. Bake for 30 to 40 minutes, basting every 10 minutes, or until fish flakes with a fork. Serve with pan juices.

TIP: If desired, recipe can be prepared without fennel.

6 servings

NUTRITION FACTS (1 serving)
Calories 200 • Protein 18 g • Carbohydrate 3 g
Fat 13 g • Cholesterol 25 mg • Sodium 260 mg

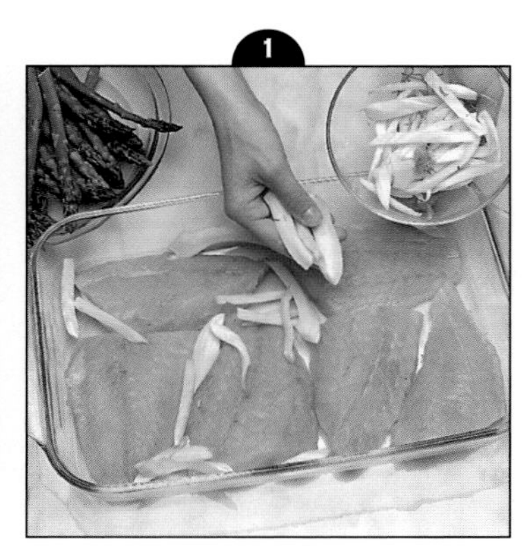

1 *Place asparagus and fennel pieces on top and around fish.*

2 *In small bowl, stir together all remaining ingredients.*

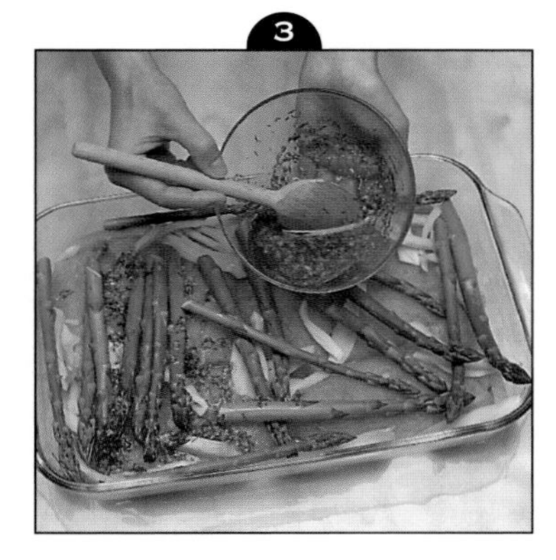

3 *Pour butter and orange mixture over fish.*

TUNA VEGETABLE À LA KING

Preparation time: 15 minutes
Cooking time: 10 minutes

¼ cup	butter	50 mL
¼ cup	chopped fresh onion	50 mL
3 tbsp	all-purpose flour	45 mL
2 cups	milk	500 mL
2	cans (6 oz/170 g each) tuna, drained, flaked	2
1	package (10 oz/284 g) frozen mixed vegetables, cooked, drained	1
½ tsp	salt	2 mL
⅛ tsp	pepper	0.5 mL
1 tsp	Worcestershire sauce	5 mL
½ cup	shredded American cheese	125 mL

- In medium saucepan, melt butter until sizzling; add onion. Cook over medium heat, stirring occasionally, until onion is softened (2 to 3 minutes).
- Stir in flour. With wire whisk, stir in milk. Continue cooking, stirring occasionally, until mixture thickens and comes to a full boil (3 to 5 minutes).
- Stir in all remaining ingredients *except* cheese. Continue cooking until mixture is heated through (3 to 4 minutes). Stir in cheese until melted (2 to 3 minutes).
- Serve on toasted English muffin, waffle, corn bread or toast.

5 servings

NUTRITION FACTS (1 serving)
Calories 360 • Protein 28 g • Carbohydrate 15 g
Fat 21 g • Cholesterol 55 mg • Sodium 810 mg

CHEESY GARDEN-STYLE FISH

Preparation time: 20 minutes
Baking time: 30 minutes

1 lb	fresh fish fillets	450 g
1	medium zucchini, cut in 2-inch (5 cm) julienne strips	1
1	medium tomato, seeded, chopped	1
3 tbsp	butter, melted	45 mL
1 tbsp	lemon juice	15 mL
1 tsp	dried basil leaves	5 mL
½ tsp	salt	2 mL
⅛ tsp	pepper	0.5 mL
½ cup	shredded Cheddar cheese	125 mL
½ cup	shredded Monterey Jack cheese	125 mL

- Heat oven to 350°F (180°C). Place fish in 13 x 9-inch (33 x 23 cm) baking pan. Place zucchini and tomato around and over fish.
- In small bowl, stir together butter, lemon juice, basil leaves, salt and pepper; pour over fish. Bake for 30 to 40 minutes or until fish flakes with a fork.
- Transfer fish and vegetables to serving platter; sprinkle with cheeses.

4 servings

NUTRITION FACTS (1 serving)
Calories 290 • Protein 28 g • Carbohydrate 4 g
Fat 19 g • Cholesterol 100 mg • Sodium 580 mg

QUICK COD VERACRUZ

Preparation time: 5 minutes
Cooking time: 16 minutes

1	can (14½ oz/411 g) Mexican-style stewed tomatoes *or* salsa-style diced tomatoes	1
1 tbsp	fresh lemon juice	15 mL
1½ lbs	fresh *or* frozen cod fillets, thawed, drained	675 g
2 tbsp	sliced ripe olives	30 mL

- In large nonstick skillet, combine tomatoes and lemon juice. Cook over medium-high heat until mixture comes to a boil (3 to 5 minutes).
- Reduce heat to medium. Cook, stirring occasionally, until sauce is reduced (8 to 10 minutes).
- Add cod fillets. Cover and continue cooking, turning once, until fish flakes with a fork (5 to 6 minutes).
- To serve, sprinkle with olives.

6 servings

NUTRITION FACTS (1 serving)
Calories 130 • Protein 21 g • Carbohydrate 7 g
Fat 1.5 g • Cholesterol 50 mg • Sodium 360 mg

SALSA VERDE FISH SAUTÉ

Preparation time: 5 minutes
Cooking time: 5 minutes

1 tbsp	butter	15 mL
1 cup	green chili salsa (salsa verde)	250 mL
1 lb	fresh *or* frozen white fish fillets, thawed	450 g
2 tbsp	chopped fresh cilantro	30 mL
	Lime slices, if desired	

- In large skillet, melt butter until sizzling; add salsa and fish. Cover and cook over medium heat, turning once, until fish flakes with a fork (5 to 6 minutes).
- Serve fish with salsa. Sprinkle with cilantro and garnish with lime slices, if desired.

4 servings

NUTRITION FACTS (1 serving)
Calories 190 • Protein 22 g • Carbohydrate 3 g
Fat 10 g • Cholesterol 75 mg • Sodium 105 mg

SALMON AND CHEESE STUFFED SHELLS

Preparation time: 25 minutes
Cooking time: 10 minutes
Baking time: 20 minutes

16	uncooked dried jumbo pasta shells	16
½ cup	Mayonnaise and Dill Blend*	125 mL
¼ cup	all-purpose flour	50 mL
2 cups	milk	500 mL
¾ cup	frozen peas, thawed	175 mL
1	can (14¾ oz/418 g) salmon, flaked, skin and bones removed	1
1 cup	cubed American cheese, ½-inch (1 cm)	250 mL

- Heat oven to 350°F (180°C). Cook shells according to package directions. Drain and rinse with cold water. Dry on paper towel. Place shells in 12 x 8-inch (30 x 20 cm) baking dish.
- Meanwhile, in medium saucepan, combine mayonnaise and flour. Gradually add milk, stirring constantly, until thickened (10 to 12 minutes). Keep warm.
- In medium bowl, stir together peas, salmon and cheese. Spoon *3 tbsp (45 mL)* mixture into each cooked shell.
- Spoon warm sauce over shells. Bake for 20 to 25 minutes or until heated through.

** Substitute ½ cup (125 mL) mayonnaise and ½ tsp (2 mL) dill weed.*

4 servings

NUTRITION FACTS (1 serving)
Calories 730 • Protein 38 g • Carbohydrate 44 g
Fat 42 g • Cholesterol 100 mg • Sodium 1280 mg

In medium saucepan, combine mayonnaise and flour. Gradually add milk, stirring constantly, until thickened.

In medium bowl, stir together peas, salmon and cheese.

Spoon 3 tbsp (45 mL) mixture into each cooked shell.

Spoon warm sauce over shells.

ORANGE ROUGHY WITH BASIL AND LEMON

Preparation time: 10 minutes
Broiling time: 10 minutes

3 tbsp	butter, softened	45 mL
½ tsp	dried basil leaves	2 mL
½ tsp	lemon pepper	2 mL
¾ lb	orange roughy *or* white fish fillets	350 g
4	lemon slices	4

- Heat broiler. In small bowl, stir together butter, basil leaves and lemon pepper. Place fillets on greased broiler pan. Spread ½ butter mixture over *one side* of fillets.
- Broil 5 to 8 inches (13 to 20 cm) from heat for 5 minutes. Turn fillets over; top with remaining butter mixture and lemon slices. Continue broiling until fish flakes with a fork (5 to 6 minutes).

4 servings

NUTRITION FACTS (1 serving)
Calories 140 • Protein 13 g • Carbohydrate 1 g
Fat 9 g • Cholesterol 40 mg • Sodium 220 mg

LINGUINE WITH SHRIMP AND PEPPERS

Preparation time: 20 minutes
Cooking time: 7 minutes

8 oz	uncooked dried linguine *or* fettucine	225 g
5 tbsp	Roasted Garlic Butter with Olive Oil	75 mL
½ lb	fresh medium shrimp, peeled, deveined, tails intact	225 g
1 cup	fresh mushrooms, sliced	250 mL
¾ cup	thin strips red pepper	175 mL
¾ cup	thin strips yellow pepper	175 mL
¼ cup	chopped fresh parsley	50 mL
½ cup	freshly grated Parmesan cheese	125 mL
	Salt	
	Pepper	

- Cook linguine according to package directions. Drain and keep warm.
- Meanwhile, in large skillet, melt 2 *tbsp (30 mL)* garlic butter until sizzling; add shrimp. Cook over medium heat, stirring occasionally, until shrimp turn pink (1 to 2 minutes). Remove shrimp; set aside.
- In same pan, melt remaining garlic butter until sizzling; add mushrooms and red and yellow peppers. Cook over medium heat, stirring occasionally, until peppers are crisply tender (5 to 7 minutes). Stir in shrimp. Continue cooking until heated through (1 to 2 minutes).
- In large serving bowl, toss together hot cooked linguine, shrimp mixture, parsley and cheese. Season with salt and pepper to taste.

6 servings

NUTRITION FACTS (1 serving)
Calories 290 • Protein 14 g • Carbohydrate 30 g
Fat 13 g • Cholesterol 65 mg • Sodium 270 mg

Meatless
Main Dishes

SPICY BLACK BEAN AND CHEESE ENCHILADAS

Preparation time:* 15 *minutes
Cooking time:* 5 *minutes
Baking time:* 18 *minutes

⅔ cup	water	150 mL
1	package (1.25 oz/35 g) dry enchilada seasoning mix	1
2	cans (15 oz/425 g each) black beans, rinsed, drained	2
1 cup	light sour cream	250 mL
8	8-inch (20 cm) flour tortillas	8
1	can (10 oz/296 mL) enchilada sauce	1
1 cup	finely shredded Cheddar cheese	250 mL
2 tbsp	sliced green onions	30 mL
	Chopped tomatoes, if desired	
	Shredded lettuce, if desired	
	Sour cream, if desired	

- Heat oven to 375°F (180°C). In large skillet, stir together water and dry enchilada seasoning mix; stir in beans. Cook over medium-high heat until mixture just comes to a boil (2 to 3 minutes).
- Reduce heat to low. Cook, stirring occasionally, until mixture thickens (3 to 4 minutes). Remove from heat; stir in *½ cup (125 mL)* sour cream.
- To assemble each tortilla, spread *1 tbsp (15 mL)* enchilada sauce on tortilla. Place *⅓ cup (75 mL)* bean mixture in center of tortilla; sprinkle with *1 tbsp (15 mL)* cheese.
- Roll up tortilla; place, seam-side down, in greased 13 x 9-inch (33 x 23 cm) baking pan. Pour remaining enchilada sauce over enchiladas. Cover with aluminum foil.
- Bake for 15 minutes or until heated through. Sprinkle with remaining cheese. Continue baking, uncovered, for 3 to 5 minutes or until cheese is melted.
- To serve, top each enchilada with a dollop of remaining sour cream; sprinkle with green onions. Serve with chopped tomato, shredded lettuce and sour cream, if desired.

8 servings

NUTRITION FACTS (1 serving)
Calories 340 • Protein 15 g • Carbohydrate 48 g
Fat 10 g • Cholesterol 20 mg • Sodium 860 mg

MUSHROOM FRITTATA WITH RED PEPPER SAUCE

Preparation time: 20 minutes
Cooking time: 16 minutes

SAUCE

½	large red pepper, chopped	½
½	jar (7¼ oz/205 g) roasted red peppers, quartered, drained	½
1 tbsp	butter	15 mL
½ tsp	finely chopped fresh garlic	2 mL
⅛ to ¼ tsp	crushed red pepper flakes	0.5 to 1 mL

FRITTATA

2 tbsp	butter	30 mL
1 cup	sliced mushrooms	250 mL
1	medium onion, chopped	1
2 tsp	finely chopped fresh garlic	10 mL
4	eggs, well-beaten	4
4	egg whites, well-beaten	4
	Salt	
	Pepper	
	Freshly grated Parmesan cheese, if desired	

- In medium saucepan, combine all sauce ingredients; mix well. Cook over medium heat, stirring occasionally, until red pepper is softened (3 to 4 minutes); set aside.
- In large skillet, melt 2 tbsp (30 mL) butter until sizzling; add mushrooms, onion and garlic. Cook over medium-high heat, stirring occasionally, until mushrooms are softened (4 to 5 minutes).
- Add eggs and egg whites. Continue cooking, lifting edges to allow eggs to flow underneath, until edges are set (6 to 8 minutes). Cover and continue cooking until top is slightly puffy and set (3 to 4 minutes).
- To serve, spoon sauce over each serving. Season to taste with salt and pepper. Sprinkle with Parmesan cheese, if desired.

6 servings

NUTRITION FACTS (1 serving)
Calories 140 • Protein 8 g • Carbohydrate 5 g
Fat 10 g • Cholesterol 140 mg • Sodium 140 mg

TOMATO AND VEGETABLE STRATA

Preparation time: 30 minutes
Chilling time: 8 hours
Baking time: 45 minutes

MUSHROOM MIXTURE

1 tbsp	olive *or* vegetable oil	15 mL
1½ cups	sliced mushrooms	375 mL
1	medium onion, chopped	1

COTTAGE CHEESE MIXTURE

1	container (16 oz/454 g) lowfat cottage cheese, well-drained	1
1	package (10 oz/284 g) frozen chopped spinach, thawed, well-drained	1
¼ tsp	ground nutmeg	1 mL
¼ tsp	coarsely ground pepper	1 mL

STRATA

1	can (16 oz/473 mL) herb and garlic chunky tomato sauce	1
½	loaf Italian *or* French bread, cut into ¼-inch (5 mm) slices	½
1 cup	shredded mozzarella cheese	250 mL
1 cup	milk	250 mL
4	eggs	4

- In medium saucepan, heat oil; add mushrooms and onion. Cook over medium-high heat, stirring occasionally, until mushrooms and onion are softened (6 to 8 minutes); set aside.
- In large bowl, combine all cottage cheese mixture ingredients; mix well. In lightly greased 12 x 8-inch (30 x 20 cm) baking dish, spread *¼ cup (50 mL)* tomato sauce. Place ½ bread slices over tomato sauce, top with cottage cheese mixture, then remaining bread slices, mushroom mixture, mozzarella cheese and remaining tomato sauce.
- In small bowl, combine milk and eggs; mix well. Slowly pour egg mixture over strata, poking with tip of knife until all mixture has been absorbed. Cover and refrigerate 8 hours or overnight.
- *Heat oven to 375°F (190°C).* Bake for 45 to 50 minutes or until knife inserted in center comes out clean and strata is puffed and golden brown. Let stand 10 minutes before serving.

8 servings

NUTRITION FACTS (1 serving)
Calories 290 • Protein 21 g • Carbohydrate 32 g
Fat 9 g • Cholesterol 95 mg • Sodium 550 mg

1

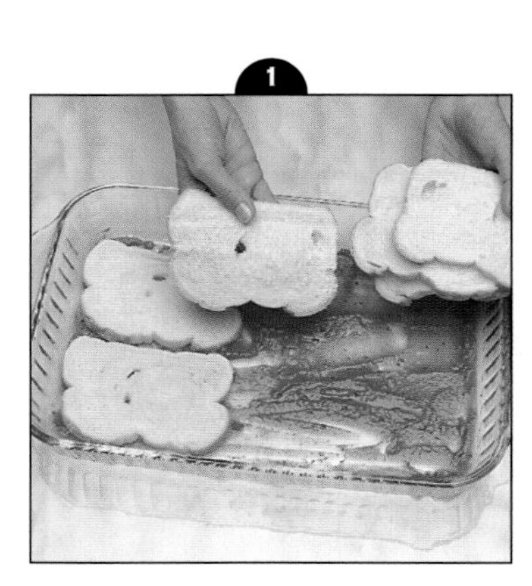

Place ½ bread slices over tomato sauce.

2

Top with cottage cheese mixture.

3

Top with remaining bread slices and mushroom mixture.

Top with mozzarella cheese and remaining tomato sauce.

In medium bowl combine milk and eggs; mix well.

Slowly pour egg mixture over strata, poking with tip of knife until all mixture has been absorbed.

MEATLESS HOPPIN' JOHN

***Preparation time:** 20 minutes*
***Cooking time:** 9 minutes*

2 tbsp	butter	30 mL
1 cup	chopped green pepper	250 mL
1 cup	chopped red pepper	250 mL
½ cup	sliced green onions	125 mL
2 tsp	finely chopped fresh garlic	10 mL
1 cup	frozen baby peas	250 mL
1	can (14½ oz/429 mL) vegetable broth	1
1	package (6¼ oz/177g) quick-cooking long grain and wild rice pilaf mix	1
1	can (15 oz/425 g) black-eyed peas, rinsed, drained	1

- In large skillet, melt butter until sizzling; add green pepper, red pepper, green onions and garlic. Cook over medium heat, stirring occasionally, until tender (3 to 4 minutes).
- Add peas, vegetable broth and pilaf mix including seasoning packet. Continue cooking, stirring occasionally, until mixture comes to a full boil (1 to 2 minutes).
- Reduce heat to low. Cover and cook until liquid is absorbed (5 to 7 minutes). Stir in black-eyed peas. Continue cooking until heated through (1 to 2 minutes).

5 servings

NUTRITION FACTS (1 serving)
Calories 280 • Protein 12 g • Carbohydrate 46 g
Fat 6 g • Cholesterol 10 mg • Sodium 830 mg

RICE PATTIES FLORENTINE

Preparation time: 35 minutes
Cooking time: 17 minutes

1¼ cups	water	300 mL
1 cup	instant brown *or* white rice	250 mL
1	medium onion, chopped	1
¼ cup	seasoned fine dry bread crumbs	50 mL
¼ cup	freshly grated Parmesan cheese	50 mL
1	package (10 oz/284 g) frozen chopped spinach, thawed, well-drained	1
1	egg, slightly beaten	1
½ cup	fat free sour cream	125 mL
½ cup	finely chopped seeded cucumber	125 mL
½ tsp	dried dill weed	2 mL
1 tbsp	butter	15 mL

- In medium saucepan, bring water to a full boil over high heat. Add rice and onion. Cover and cook over medium-low heat until water is absorbed (8 to 10 minutes). Stir in bread crumbs, Parmesan cheese, spinach and egg. Let cool slightly.
- Shape rice mixture into four ¾-inch (2 cm) thick patties. Chill in freezer for 15 minutes.
- Meanwhile, in small bowl stir together sour cream, cucumber and dill weed. Cover and refrigerate until serving time.
- In large nonstick skillet, melt butter until sizzling; add patties. Cook over medium heat, turning once, until lightly browned (6 to 8 minutes). Serve patties with sour cream mixture.

2 servings

NUTRITION FACTS (1 serving)
Calories 610 • Protein 24 g • Carbohydrate 94 g
Fat 17 g • Cholesterol 115 mg • Sodium 500 mg

CHILI AND CHEESE TOPPED POTATOES

***Preparation time:** 5 minutes*
***Cooking time:** 15 minutes*

1	can (15½ oz/439 g) kidney beans, rinsed, drained	1
1	can (14½ oz/429 mL) chili-style *or* Mexican-style diced tomatoes	1
4	medium hot baked potatoes	4
¼ cup	shredded Cheddar *or* Chedarella® cheese	50 mL
¼ cup	sour cream (regular, light *or* fat free)	50 mL

- In medium saucepan, combine beans and tomatoes. Cook over high heat until mixture just comes to a boil (3 to 5 minutes). Reduce heat to medium. Cook, stirring occasionally, until liquid is reduced and mixture is thickened (12 to 15 minutes).
- To serve, cut open hot baked potatoes; spoon about *½ cup (125 mL)* bean mixture over each. Sprinkle each with *1 tbsp (15 mL)* cheese; dollop with *1 tbsp (15 mL)* sour cream.

4 servings

NUTRITION FACTS (1 serving)
Calories 380 • Protein 14 g • Carbohydrate 75 g
Fat 4 g • Cholesterol 10 mg • Sodium 2610 mg

MEXICAN SKILLET SUPPER

***Preparation time:** 15 minutes*
***Cooking time:** 32 minutes*

1	small jalapeño pepper, cut in half crosswise, seeded, sliced	1
1 tbsp	vegetable oil	15 mL
1	medium onion, chopped	1
1¾ cups	water	425 mL
1 cup	uncooked long grain rice	250 mL
2	cans (16 oz/454 g each) chili hot beans	2
1	can (4 oz/113 g) chopped green chilies	1
½ tsp	salt	2 mL
½ cup	shredded Cheddar cheese	125 mL
½ cup	chopped tomato	125 mL
¼ cup	thinly sliced green onions	50 mL

- *Reserve half of jalapeño pepper slices for garnish.* Finely chop remaining slices. In large skillet, heat oil; add chopped jalapeño and onion. Cook over medium-high heat, stirring occasionally, until onion is crisply tender (2 to 3 minutes).
- Add water, rice, beans, chilies and salt. Continue cooking until mixture just comes to a boil (3 to 5 minutes).
- Reduce heat to medium-low. Cover and cook, stirring occasionally, until rice is tender and liquid is absorbed (25 to 30 minutes).
- Remove from heat. Sprinkle with cheese. Cover and let stand until cheese is melted (2 to 3 minutes). Garnish with reserved jalapeño slices, tomato and green onions.

6 servings

NUTRITION FACTS (1 serving)
Calories 380 • Protein 14 g • Carbohydrate 51 g
Fat 14 g • Cholesterol 35 mg • Sodium 1250 mg

ARTICHOKE AND MUSHROOM RISOTTO

***Preparation time:* 5 minutes**
***Cooking time:* 31 minutes**

2	cans (14½ oz/429 mL each) chicken broth	2
1 tbsp	butter	15 mL
1 cup	uncooked Arborio rice	250 mL
1 cup	thinly sliced fresh mushrooms	250 mL
1	package (9 oz/255 g) frozen artichoke hearts, thawed, drained, cut into quarters	1
1 tbsp	lemon juice	15 mL
2 tbsp	freshly shredded Parmesan cheese, if desired	30 mL

- In medium saucepan, cook chicken broth until boiling (4 to 6 minutes). Reduce heat to low and keep warm.
- Meanwhile, in large skillet, melt butter until sizzling; add rice. Cook over medium-high heat, stirring constantly, 3 minutes.
- Reduce heat to medium. Slowly add *1 cup (250 mL)* hot broth and mushrooms. Cook, stirring constantly, until almost all broth has been absorbed (2 to 4 minutes).
- Continue cooking, adding additional broth about *½ cup (125 mL)* at a time, stirring constantly after each addition, until broth is absorbed (4 to 5 minutes for each addition totaling 20 to 25 minutes).
- When rice is tender but firm, stir in artichoke hearts and lemon juice. Continue cooking until heated through (2 to 3 minutes). Sprinkle with cheese.

TIP: Arborio rice is an Italian short grain rice. It is traditionally used for risotto because its high starch level produces a creamy texture.

4 servings

NUTRITION FACTS (1 serving)
Calories 270 • Protein 9 g • Carbohydrate 46 g
Fat 5 g • Cholesterol 10 mg • Sodium 720 mg

1

In large skillet, melt butter until sizzling; add rice.

2

Slowly add 1 cup (250 mL) hot broth and mushrooms.

3

Add additional broth about ½ cup (125 mL) at a time, stirring constantly after each addition, until broth is absorbed.

Stir in artichoke hearts and lemon juice.

Sprinkle with cheese.

WAGON WHEEL PASTA, CHEESE AND VEGETABLES

Preparation time: 15 minutes
Baking time: 25 minutes

1 cup	**uncooked dried tri-colored wagon wheel pasta**	**250 mL**
¼ cup	**milk**	**50 mL**
1½ cups	**cubed American cheese**	**375 mL**
1	**package (16 oz/454 g) frozen vegetable combination (green beans, onions, peppers and potatoes)**	**1**
2 tbsp	**butter, melted**	**30 mL**

- Heat oven to 350°F (180°C). Cook pasta according to package directions. Drain.
- In greased medium casserole, stir together cooked pasta and all remaining ingredients.
- Bake for 25 to 30 minutes, stirring once, until heated through.

4 servings

NUTRITION FACTS (1 serving)
Calories 380 • Protein 14 g • Carbohydrate 33 g
Fat 22 g • Cholesterol 55 mg • Sodium 700 mg

PRIMAVERA PASTA

Preparation time: 15 minutes
Cooking time: 27 minutes

2 tbsp	**butter**	**30 mL**
1	**medium onion, chopped**	**1**
2 tsp	**finely chopped fresh garlic**	**10 mL**
1 cup	**sliced mushrooms**	**250 mL**
1	**small yellow squash, sliced ¼-inch (5 mm)**	**1**
1	**small zucchini, sliced ¼-inch (5 mm)**	**1**
1½ cups	**spaghetti sauce**	**375 mL**
2 tbsp	**chopped fresh oregano leaves***	**30 mL**
8 oz	**uncooked dried linguine**	**225 g**
	Freshly grated Parmesan cheese	

- In Dutch oven, melt butter until sizzling; add onion and garlic. Cook over medium heat, stirring occasionally, until onion is softened (4 to 5 minutes).
- Add mushrooms, squash and zucchini. Continue cooking, stirring occasionally, until vegetables are softened (8 to 10 minutes).
- Add spaghetti sauce and oregano. Continue cooking, stirring occasionally, until heated through and flavors are blended (15 to 18 minutes).
- Meanwhile, cook linguine according to package directions. Drain. Serve sauce over hot linguine; sprinkle with Parmesan cheese.

** Substitute 2 tsp (10 mL) dried oregano leaves.*

4 servings

NUTRITION FACTS (1 serving)
Calories 350 • Protein 10 g • Carbohydrate 56 g
Fat 10 g • Cholesterol 15 mg • Sodium 760 mg

SPANISH SKILLET CASSEROLE

***Preparation time:** 10 minutes*
***Cooking time:** 12 minutes*

1	**package (7 oz/198 g) uncooked dried elbow macaroni**	**1**
½ cup	**milk**	**125 mL**
1	**egg**	**1**
1	**can (4 oz/113 g) chopped green chilies, drained**	**1**
1 tbsp	**butter**	**15 mL**
1 cup	**shredded Hot Pepper Monterey Jack Cheese**	**250 mL**
1	**can (15 oz/425 g) pinto beans, rinsed, drained**	**1**
1 cup	**fresh chunky salsa**	**250 mL**
	Sour cream (regular, light *or* fat free), if desired	

- Cook macaroni according to package directions. Drain. Set aside.
- Meanwhile, in medium bowl, beat milk and egg together with fork. Stir in cooked macaroni and chilies.
- In large nonstick skillet, melt butter until sizzling; add macaroni mixture. Cover and cook over low heat until set (12 to 15 minutes). Remove from heat; let stand 5 minutes.
- Invert onto large serving plate or spoon onto individual plates. Top with cheese, beans and salsa. Dollop with sour cream, if desired.

6 servings

NUTRITION FACTS (1 serving)
Calories 310 • Protein 14 g • Carbohydrate 40 g
Fat 10 g • Cholesterol 55 mg • Sodium 820 mg

RAVIOLI ANTIPASTO SALAD

Preparation time: 30 minutes
Chilling time: 2 hours

1	package (9 oz/255 g) fresh cheese *or* meat-filled ravioli	1
2 cups	cubed Chedarella® *or* Cheddar cheese	500 mL
1 cup	medium pitted ripe olives	250 mL
½ cup	Italian dressing	125 mL
1	medium carrot, sliced ⅛-inch (3 mm)	1
1	medium red *or* green pepper, cubed ¾-inch (2 cm)	1
1	package (9 oz/255 g) frozen artichoke hearts, cooked, quartered, drained*	1

- Cook ravioli according to package directions. Rinse with cold water; drain.
- In large bowl, combine ravioli and all remaining ingredients; toss lightly. Cover and refrigerate at least 2 hours.

* *Substitute 1 can (14 oz/397 g) artichoke hearts, drained, cut in half.*

6 servings

NUTRITION FACTS (1 serving)
Calories 410 • Protein 17 g • Carbohydrate 24 g
Fat 28 g • Cholesterol 70 mg • Sodium 770 mg

Southwestern Vegetarian Pizza

Preparation time: 15 minutes
Baking time: 10 minutes

1	**round prebaked Italian bread shell (10 oz/284 g)**	**1**
½ cup	**sour cream (fat free *or* light)**	**125 mL**
¾ cup	**thick and chunky salsa**	**175 mL**
½ cup	**black beans, rinsed, drained**	**125 mL**
¼ cup	**sliced green onions**	**50 mL**
1 cup	**shredded Chedarella® cheese**	**250 mL**

- Heat oven to 450°F (230°C). Place bread shell on baking sheet. Spread sour cream over bread shell; top with salsa. Top with beans and green onions; sprinkle with cheese.
- Bake for 10 to 12 minutes or until cheese is melted.

TIP: To make individual pizzas, use four 7-inch (18 cm) pita breads.

4 servings

NUTRITION FACTS (1 serving)
Calories 330 • Protein 19 g • Carbohydrate 47 g
Fat 8 g • Cholesterol 20 mg • Sodium 640 mg

Bean, Cheese and Corn Burritos

Preparation time: 10 minutes
Cooking time: 5 minutes

1	**can (16 oz/454 g) chili beans**	**1**
1	**can (11 oz/312 g) whole kernel corn with red and green peppers**	**1**
½ cup	**shredded Cheddar cheese**	**125 mL**
4	**7-inch (18 cm) flour tortillas**	**4**
	Salsa, if desired	
	Sour cream (regular, light *or* fat free), if desired	
	Fresh cilantro, if desired	

- In medium saucepan, stir together beans and corn. Cook over medium-high heat, stirring occasionally, until heated through (5 to 6 minutes). Stir in cheese.
- Meanwhile, warm tortillas according to package directions. Place ¼ filling down center of each warmed tortilla; roll up. Place on serving plate; top with salsa and sour cream. Garnish with fresh cilantro, if desired.

4 servings

NUTRITION FACTS (1 serving)
Calories 370 • Protein 15 g • Carbohydrate 48 g
Fat 14 g • Cholesterol 35 mg • Sodium 1130 mg

ITALIAN PASTA AND SPINACH CASSEROLE

Preparation time: 20 minutes
Baking time: 30 minutes

8 oz	uncooked dried spaghetti	225 g
2 cups	shredded mozzarella cheese	500 mL
1½ cups	sour cream (regular, light *or* fat free)	375 mL
1	package (10 oz/284 g) frozen chopped spinach, thawed, well-drained	1
1	egg	1
1 tsp	garlic salt	5 mL
2 cups	spaghetti sauce	500 mL

- Heat oven to 350°F (180°C). Cook spaghetti according to package directions. Drain.
- Meanwhile, in large bowl, combine all remaining ingredients *except* spaghetti sauce; stir in hot cooked spaghetti.
- Place spaghetti mixture in 12 x 8-inch (30 x 20 cm) baking dish; pour spaghetti sauce evenly over mixture. Bake for 30 to 40 minutes or until heated through.

12 servings

NUTRITION FACTS (1 serving)
Calories 215 • Protein 11 g • Carbohydrate 26 g
Fat 8 g • Cholesterol 35 mg • Sodium 520 mg

HERB GARDEN AND LEMON PASTA

Preparation time: 20 minutes
Cooking time: 7 minutes

8 oz	uncooked dried rotini (corkscrew *or* pasta twists)	225 g
3 tbsp	butter	45 mL
1 cup	chopped red onion	250 mL
3	medium zucchini, sliced ¼-inch (5 mm)	3
¼ cup	freshly grated Parmesan cheese	50 mL
¼ cup	chopped fresh basil leaves	50 mL
¼ cup	chopped fresh chives	50 mL
¼ cup	chopped fresh parsley	50 mL
2	medium tomatoes, cut into wedges	2
2 tbsp	lemon juice	30 mL
½ tsp	salt	2 mL
¼ tsp	pepper	1 mL

- Cook rotini according to package directions. Drain.
- Meanwhile, in large skillet, melt butter until sizzling; add onion and zucchini. Cook over medium heat, stirring occasionally, until zucchini is crisply tender (5 to 7 minutes).
- Add cooked rotini and all remaining ingredients. Cover and let stand until tomatoes are heated through (2 to 3 minutes).

6 servings

NUTRITION FACTS (1 serving)
Calories 240 • Protein 8 g • Carbohydrate 35 g
Fat 8 g • Cholesterol 20 mg • Sodium 320 mg

STUFFED SWEET PEPPERS

Preparation time: 30 minutes
Cooking time: 43 minutes

2 tbsp	olive or vegetable oil	30 mL
½ cup	shredded carrot	125 mL
½ cup	sliced mushrooms	125 mL
½ cup	chopped onion	125 mL
½ cup	shredded zucchini	125 mL
1 tsp	finely chopped fresh garlic	5 mL
1 cup	cooked long grain rice	250 mL
1	container (15 oz/425 g) lowfat ricotta cheese, drained	1
1	egg, slightly beaten	1
2 tbsp	chopped fresh basil leaves*	30 mL
½ tsp	salt	2 mL
4	medium green peppers, cut in half lengthwise, stems and seeds removed	4
1	can (8 oz/237 mL) tomato sauce	1
½ cup	shredded mozzarella cheese	125 mL

- Heat oven to 350°F (180°C). In medium saucepan, heat oil; add carrot, mushrooms, onion, zucchini and garlic. Cook over medium heat, stirring occasionally, until vegetables are softened (6 to 8 minutes). Set aside.
- In large bowl, combine rice, ricotta cheese, egg, basil and salt; mix well. Stir in carrot mixture.
- Place about ½ *cup (125 mL)* vegetable cheese mixture into each green pepper half. In 12 x 8-inch (30 x 20 cm) baking dish, spread ½ *cup (125 mL)* tomato sauce; place green peppers over sauce. Pour remaining tomato sauce over green peppers.
- Cover and bake for 40 to 45 minutes or until filling is hot and green peppers are softened. Uncover and sprinkle with cheese. Continue baking for 3 to 5 minutes or until cheese is melted.

** Substitute 1½ tsp (7 mL) dried basil leaves.*

4 servings

NUTRITION FACTS (1 serving)
Calories 360 • Protein 21 g • Carbohydrate 28 g
Fat 19 g • Cholesterol 95 mg • Sodium 900 mg

1

In medium saucepan, heat oil; add carrot, mushrooms, onion, zucchini and garlic.

2

In large bowl, combine rice, ricotta cheese, egg, basil and salt; mix well.

3

Stir in carrot mixture.

4

Place about ½ cup (125 mL) vegetable-cheese mixture into each green pepper half.

5

Pour remaining tomato sauce over green peppers.

6

Uncover baking dish and sprinkle with cheese.

30 Minutes
or Less

PEPPERONI GARDEN SKILLET

Preparation time: 20 minutes
Cooking time: 7 minutes

¼ cup	butter	50 mL
2 cups	broccoli florets	500 mL
2	medium carrots, sliced diagonally ¼-inch (5 mm)	2
1	medium onion, cut into ¼-inch (5 mm) rings	1
1 tsp	Italian seasoning*	5 mL
1 cup	sliced fresh mushrooms, ¼-inch (5 mm)	250 mL
1	green *or* red pepper, cut into strips	1
½ cup	sliced pepperoni	125 mL
1 cup	shredded Chedarella® cheese	250 mL

- In large deep skillet, melt butter until sizzling; add broccoli, carrots, onion and Italian seasoning. Cook over medium heat, stirring constantly, until vegetables are crisply tender (5 to 6 minutes).
- Stir in mushrooms, green pepper and pepperoni. Continue cooking, stirring constantly, until green pepper is crisply tender (2 to 3 minutes).
- Remove from heat. Sprinkle cheese over vegetables. Cover and let stand until cheese is melted (1 to 2 minutes).

** Substitute ¼ tsp (1 mL)* each *dried oregano, marjoram and basil leaves, and ⅛ tsp (0.5 mL) rubbed sage.*

4 servings

NUTRITION FACTS (1 serving)
Calories 340 • Protein 13 g • Carbohydrate 12 g
Fat 27 g • Cholesterol 70 mg • Sodium 710 mg

ITALIAN HERB CHICKEN

Preparation time: 10 minutes
Grilling time: 15 minutes

2 tbsp	**Roasted Garlic Butter with Olive Oil, melted***	**30 mL**
1 tsp	**Italian seasoning****	**5 mL**
¼ tsp	**salt**	**1 mL**
⅛ tsp	**pepper**	**0.5 mL**
4	**boneless skinless chicken breasts, about 4 oz (115 g) each**	**4**

- Heat gas grill on medium *or* charcoal grill until coals are ash white. Make aluminum foil drip pan; place opposite coals.
- In small bowl, stir together all ingredients *except* chicken. Brush butter mixture over chicken. Place chicken on grill over drip pan. Grill, turning occasionally, until chicken is no longer pink (15 to 20 minutes).

** Substitute 2 tbsp (30 mL) butter and 2 tsp (10 mL) finely chopped fresh garlic.*

*** Substitute ¼ tsp (1 mL) each dried oregano, marjoram and basil leaves, and ⅛ tsp (0.5 mL) rubbed sage.*

4 servings

NUTRITION FACTS (1 serving)
Calories 180 • Protein 27 g • Carbohydrate 0 g
Fat 7 g • Cholesterol 80 mg • Sodium 400 mg

ITALIAN SKILLET DINNER

Preparation time: 10 minutes
Cooking time: 15 minutes

1 lb	**Italian sausage *or* ground beef**	**450 g**
½ cup	**chopped green pepper**	**125 mL**
1	**medium onion, chopped**	**1**
1½ cups	**vegetable tomato juice *or* tomato juice**	**375 mL**
1	**can (14½ oz/429 mL) diced tomatoes**	**1**
1½ cups	**uncooked instant rice**	**375 mL**
1 cup	**shredded mozzarella cheese**	**250 mL**

- In large skillet, cook Italian sausage over medium heat, stirring occasionally, until sausage is no longer pink (4 to 6 minutes). Drain off fat.
- Add green pepper and onion. Continue cooking until green pepper is crisply tender (2 to 3 minutes). Stir in tomato juice and tomatoes. Continue cooking, stirring occasionally, until mixture comes to a full boil (2 to 3 minutes). Remove from heat; stir in rice.
- Cover and let stand until liquid is absorbed (6 to 8 minutes). Sprinkle with cheese. Cover and let stand until cheese is melted (1 to 2 minutes).

6 servings

NUTRITION FACTS (1 serving)
Calories 360 • Protein 19 g • Carbohydrate 29 g
Fat 18 g • Cholesterol 55 mg • Sodium 980 mg

BUTTER-CRUSTED HERBED FISH

Preparation time: 10 minutes
Cooking time: 10 minutes

¼ cup	**all-purpose flour**	**50 mL**
2 tbsp	**yellow corn meal**	**30 mL**
1 tsp	**dried basil leaves**	**5 mL**
1 tsp	**dried thyme leaves**	**5 mL**
¼ tsp	**salt**	**1 mL**
¼ tsp	**pepper**	**1 mL**
¼ cup	**milk**	**50 mL**
¼ cup	**butter**	**50 mL**
1 lb	**Northern *or* Walleye fillets**	**450 g**
	Lemon wedges, if desired	

- In pie pan, combine flour, corn meal, thyme, basil, salt and pepper.
- In medium bowl, pour milk. Dip fish in milk; then coat with flour mixture. Repeat.
- In large heavy skillet, melt butter until sizzling; add fish. Cook over medium-high heat for 5 minutes; turn. Continue cooking until golden brown (5 to 6 minutes).
- Garnish with lemon wedges, if desired. Serve immediately.

4 servings

NUTRITION FACTS (1 serving)
Calories 260 • Protein 24 g • Carbohydrate 11 g
Fat 13 g • Cholesterol 75 mg • Sodium 300 mg

Dip fish in milk.

Coat fish with flour mixture.

Cook fish over medium-high heat for 5 minutes; turn. Continue cooking until golden brown.

EASY STROGANOFF

Preparation time: 10 minutes
Cooking time: 12 minutes

⅓ cup	finely chopped onion	75 mL
1 lb	ground beef	450 g
3 tbsp	all-purpose flour	45 mL
½ cup	water	125 mL
1	can (4 oz/113 g) mushroom stems and pieces	1
1 tsp	finely chopped fresh garlic	5 mL
½ tsp	salt	2 mL
1 cup	sour cream (regular, light *or* fat free)	250 mL
	Hot cooked egg noodles	
	Chopped fresh parsley	

- In large skillet, cook onion and ground beef over medium-high heat, stirring occasionally, until browned (5 to 7 minutes). Drain off fat.
- Stir flour into beef mixture. Add water, mushrooms, garlic and salt. Cook, stirring constantly, until mixture thickens (3 to 4 minutes). Reduce heat to low. Stir in sour cream; cook until heated through (4 to 5 minutes).
- To serve, spoon beef mixture over cooked noodles. Garnish with parsley.

4 servings

NUTRITION FACTS (1 serving)
Calories 360 • Protein 23 g • Carbohydrate 11 g
Fat 24 g • Cholesterol 100 mg • Sodium 480 mg

PEPPER CHICKEN PASTA

Preparation time: 15 minutes
Cooking time: 6 minutes

8 oz	uncooked dried rotini (corkscrew *or* pasta twists)	225 g
1 tbsp	Roasted Garlic Butter with Olive Oil*	15 mL
1 lb	boneless skinless chicken breast tenders**	450 g
1	medium yellow pepper, cut into thin strips	1
1	jar (14 oz/414 mL) garden-style spaghetti sauce	1
½ cup	shredded Monterey Jack *or* mozzarella cheese	125 mL
	Fresh basil leaves, if desired	

- Cook rotini according to package directions. Drain; keep warm.
- Meanwhile, in large nonstick skillet, melt garlic butter; add chicken. Cook over medium-high heat, turning occasionally, until golden brown on all sides (3 to 5 minutes).
- Add peppers and continue cooking until peppers are tender (2 to 4 minutes). Stir in spaghetti sauce; continue cooking until heated through (1 to 2 minutes).
- Serve over warm rotini. Sprinkle with cheese and garnish with fresh basil, if desired.

** Substitute 1 tbsp (15 mL) butter, softened, and 2 tsp (10 mL) finely chopped fresh garlic.*

*** Substitute 1 lb (450 g) boneless skinless chicken breast halves, cut into strips.*

6 servings

NUTRITION FACTS (1 serving)
Calories 340 • Protein 24 g • Carbohydrate 37 g
Fat 9 g • Cholesterol 60 mg • Sodium 360 mg

SESAME CHICKEN BREASTS

Preparation time: 5 minutes
Cooking time: 13 minutes

2 tbsp	**butter**	**30 mL**
1 tsp	**finely chopped fresh garlic**	**5 mL**
4	**boneless skinless chicken breasts, about 6 oz (170 g) each**	**4**
2 tsp	**sesame seeds, toasted**	**10 mL**
1 tbsp	**chopped fresh parsley**	**15 mL**
	Salt	
	Pepper	

- In large nonstick skillet, melt butter until sizzling; stir in garlic. Add chicken breasts. Cook over medium heat, turning occasionally, until golden brown (12 to 15 minutes).
- Sprinkle with sesame seeds. Continue cooking until chicken is no longer pink (1 to 2 minutes). Sprinkle with parsley. Season with salt and pepper to taste.

Grilling Directions: Prepare grill placing coals to one side; heat until coals are ash white. Make aluminum foil drip pan; place opposite coals. Meanwhile, combine *melted* butter, garlic, sesame seeds and parsley. Place chicken breasts on grill over drip pan. Grill, turning and brushing with butter mixture occasionally, until chicken is no longer pink (12 to 15 minutes).

Broiling Directions: Heat broiler. Meanwhile, combine *melted* butter, garlic, sesame seeds and parsley. Place chicken breasts on greased broiler pan. Broil 4 to 6 inches (10 to 15 cm) from heat, turning every 5 minutes and basting with butter mixture, until chicken is no longer pink (15 to 20 minutes).

4 servings

NUTRITION FACTS (1 serving)
Calories 260 • Protein 40 g • Carbohydrate 0 g
Fat 9 g • Cholesterol 115 mg • Sodium 180 mg

SAUCY CHICKEN AND VEGETABLES OVER FETTUCCINE

Preparation time: 10 minutes
Cooking time: 10 minutes

6 oz	uncooked dried fettuccine	170 g
2 tbsp	butter	30 mL
1 lb	boneless skinless chicken breasts, cut into ½-inch (1 cm) strips	450 g
2 tbsp	chopped green onions	30 mL
1	package (16 oz/454 g) pre-cut fresh stir-fry vegetables, coarsely chopped	1
1 cup	sour cream (regular, light *or* fat free)	250 mL
⅓ cup	chicken broth	75 mL
	Coarsely ground pepper	

- Cook fettuccine according to package directions. Drain; keep warm.
- Meanwhile, in large nonstick skillet, melt butter until sizzling; add chicken and green onions. Cook over medium heat, stirring occasionally, 4 minutes.
- Add vegetables and continue cooking, stirring occasionally, until vegetables are crisply tender (4 to 6 minutes). Stir in sour cream and chicken broth. Continue cooking until heated through (1 to 2 minutes).
- Serve sauce over hot fettuccine. Garnish with coarsely ground pepper.

4 servings

NUTRITION FACTS (1 serving)
Calories 500 • Protein 36 g • Carbohydrate 43 g
Fat 20 g • Cholesterol 115 mg • Sodium 260 mg

DEVILED STEAK BROIL

Preparation time: 5 minutes
Broiling time: 10 minutes

½ tsp	coarsely ground pepper	2 mL
⅛ tsp	garlic powder	0.5 mL
⅛ tsp	ground red pepper	0.5 mL
2 tbsp	country-style Dijon mustard	30 mL
1½ lbs	boneless beef sirloin steak, about 1 inch (2.5 cm) thick	675 g

- Heat broiler. In small bowl, combine all ingredients *except* steak; mix well. Set aside.
- Place steak on broiler pan. Broil 4 to 6 inches (10 to 15 cm) from heat for 4 minutes; turn. Spread mustard mixture on steak. Continue broiling until cooked as desired (6 to 8 minutes).

6 servings

NUTRITION FACTS (1 serving)
Calories 150 • Protein 24 g • Carbohydrate 1 g
Fat 5 g • Cholesterol 70 mg • Sodium 190 mg

SALSA AND CHEESE STUFFED BURGERS

***Preparation time:* 10 minutes**
***Broiling time:* 10 minutes**

½ cup	**thick and chunky salsa**	**125 mL**
1 lb	**lean ground beef**	**450 g**
3 tbsp	**finely chopped onion**	**45 mL**
2 tsp	**chili powder**	**10 mL**
½ tsp	**salt**	**2 mL**
½ tsp	**ground cumin**	**2 mL**
¼ tsp	**pepper**	**1 mL**
¼ cup	**cubed Cheddar cheese, ½-inch (1 cm)**	**50 mL**
	Shredded lettuce, salsa *and/or* guacamole, if desired	

- Heat broiler. In medium bowl, lightly mix ½ cup (125 mL) salsa, ground beef, onion, chili powder, salt, cumin and pepper. Shape into eight ½-inch (1 cm) thick patties.
- Place *1 cube* cheese in center of each of 4 patties. Top each with another patty; seal edges.
- *Heat broiler.* Spray broiler pan with no stick cooking spray. Place patties on pan. Broil 4 to 6 inches (10 to 15 cm) from heat, turning once, until cooked as desired (10 to 12 minutes). Top with lettuce, salsa *and/or* guacamole, if desired.

TIP: If desired, grill burgers instead of broiling.

4 servings

NUTRITION FACTS (1 burger)
Calories 340 • Protein 22 g • Carbohydrate 3 g
Fat 26 g • Cholesterol 90 mg • Sodium 520 mg

BEEF AND CHILI TOSS

***Preparation time:* 15 minutes**
***Cooking time:* 6 minutes**

PASTA

5 oz	**uncooked dried fettuccine**	**140 g**

BEEF

2 tsp	**olive *or* vegetable oil**	**10 mL**
1½ tsp	**purchased minced garlic**	**7 mL**
1 lb	**beef sirloin, cut into ½-inch (1 cm) strips**	**450 g**
2 tsp	**chili powder**	**10 mL**
1	**green pepper, cut into 2 x ½-inch (5 x 1 cm) strips**	**1**
1	**can (4 oz/113 g) chopped green chilies**	**1**
	Salt	
	Pepper	

- Cook fettuccine according to package directions. Drain.
- Meanwhile, in large skillet, heat oil; add garlic. Cook over medium-high heat, stirring constantly, 1 minute. Stir in beef and chili powder. Continue cooking, stirring occasionally, until beef is lightly browned (2 to 3 minutes).
- Stir in all remaining ingredients except cooked fettucine. Continue cooking, stirring occasionally, until pepper is crisply tender (3 to 5 minutes). Stir in cooked fettuccine; continue cooking until heated through (1 minute). Season to taste with salt and pepper.

4 servings

NUTRITION FACTS (1 serving)
Calories 320 • Protein 29 g • Carbohydrate 31 g
Fat 8 g • Cholesterol 70 mg • Sodium 410 mg

SHORT-CUT SHRIMP JAMBALAYA

Preparation time: 10 minutes
Cooking time: 18 minutes

¼ cup	butter	50 mL
¾ cup	chopped onion	175 mL
1 cup	cubed ham, ½-inch (1 cm)	250 mL
2 tbsp	all-purpose flour	30 mL
½ tsp	salt	2 mL
1 tsp	Cajun seasoning	5 mL
2	bay leaves	2
1	can (14½ oz/411 g) stewed tomatoes	1
1½ cups	water	375 mL
2 tbsp	chili sauce	30 mL
2 cups	uncooked instant rice	500 mL
1 lb	frozen medium shrimp, thawed	450 g

- In large skillet, melt butter until sizzling; add onion and ham. Cook over medium heat, stirring occasionally, until onion is softened (5 to 7 minutes).
- Stir in flour until smooth. Add seasonings, tomatoes, water and chili sauce. Continue cooking, stirring occasionally, until mixture comes to a boil (3 to 5 minutes).
- Stir in rice and shrimp. Cover and continue cooking until rice is tender and shrimp turn pink (10 to 15 minutes). Remove bay leaves.

6 servings

NUTRITION FACTS (1 serving)
Calories 320 • Protein 24 g • Carbohydrate 33 g
Fat 10 g • Cholesterol 180 mg • Sodium 950 mg

Stir flour into onion and ham until smooth.

Add seasonings, tomatoes, water and chili sauce.

Stir in rice and shrimp. Cover and continue cooking until rice is tender and shrimp turn pink.

REVVED-UP RAVIOLI

Preparation time: 15 minutes
Cooking time: 15 minutes

1	bag (25 oz/709 g) frozen beef-filled ravioli*	1
1	bag (16 oz/454 g) frozen vegetable combination (green beans, red pepper, broccoli)	1
1 cup	fat free skim milk	250 mL
¾ cup	sour cream (light *or* fat free)	175 mL
1	package (1½ oz/42.5 g) four-cheese pasta sauce mix	1
1 tbsp	butter	15 mL

- Cook ravioli and vegetables together according to ravioli package directions. Drain; keep warm.
- Meanwhile, in small saucepan, stir together milk, sour cream and sauce mix until smooth. Cook over medium heat, stirring constantly, until mixture just comes to a boil (2 to 3 minutes). Reduce heat to low; stir in butter. Continue cooking until smooth (30 seconds).
- To serve, pour hot sauce over ravioli and vegetables.

** Substitute two 9-oz (255 g) packages fresh beef-filled ravioli.*

6 servings

NUTRITION FACTS (1 serving)
Calories 350 • Protein 16 g • Carbohydrate 50 g
Fat 10 g • Cholesterol 45 mg • Sodium 750 mg

TURKEY CURRY WITH FETTUCCINE

Preparation time: 10 minutes
Cooking time: 11 minutes

9 oz	uncooked fresh spinach fettuccine	255 g
1 lb	fresh turkey breast *or* turkey tenderloin slices, ¼-inch (5 mm) thick	450 g
1	package (16 oz/454 g) frozen vegetable combination (broccoli, cauliflower, sugar snap peas and red pepper), partially thawed	1
1 cup	sour cream (regular, light *or* fat free)	250 mL
⅓ cup	light coconut milk *or* coconut milk*	75 mL
2 tsp	curry powder	10 mL
	Salt and pepper	

- Cook fettuccine according to package directions. Drain; keep warm.
- Meanwhile, spray large skillet with no stick cooking spray. Cook turkey slices over medium heat, turning once, until lightly browned (6 to 8 minutes).
- Add vegetables. Cover and continue cooking until vegetables are crisply tender (4 to 5 minutes).
- In small bowl, stir together sour cream, coconut milk and curry powder. Gently stir sauce into meat and vegetables in skillet. Cook, stirring constantly, until heated through (1 to 2 minutes). Serve over hot cooked fettuccine. Season with salt and pepper.

** Substitute ⅓ cup (75 mL) milk plus ⅛ tsp (0.5 mL) coconut extract.*

4 servings

NUTRITION FACTS (1 serving)
Calories 550 • Protein 41 g • Carbohydrate 58 g
Fat 17 g • Cholesterol 105 mg • Sodium 115 mg

HERBED VEGETABLES AND CHICKEN

Preparation time: 10 minutes
Cooking time: 4 minutes

2 cups	frozen vegetable combination	500 mL
2 cups	cubed cooked chicken	500 mL
½ cup	light sour cream	125 mL
½ tsp	dried thyme leaves	2 mL
4	hot baked potatoes, cooked rice *or* toasted English muffins	4
1 cup	finely shredded mozzarella cheese	250 mL

- In large saucepan, prepare vegetables according to package directions. Drain.
- Add chicken, sour cream and thyme to vegetables. Cook over medium heat until heated through (4 to 6 minutes).
- To serve, spoon chicken and vegetable mixture over hot baked potatoes, cooked rice or toasted English muffins. Sprinkle each serving with *¼ cup (50 mL)* cheese.

4 servings

NUTRITION FACTS (1 serving)
Calories 390 • Protein 31 g • Carbohydrate 38 g
Fat 12 g • Cholesterol 80 mg • Sodium 290 mg

SKILLET PORK, RICE AND BEANS

Preparation time: 15 minutes
Cooking time: 10 minutes

1 tbsp	butter	15 mL
½ tsp	finely chopped fresh garlic	2 mL
1½ cups	small broccoli florets	375 mL
½ lb	pork cutlets *or* tenderloin, cut into ½-inch (1 cm) pieces	225 g
3 cups	cooked rice	750 mL
1	can (15 oz/425 g) red beans, rinsed, drained	1
3 tbsp	soy sauce	45 mL

- In large nonstick skillet, melt butter until sizzling; add garlic. Cook 1 minute. Add broccoli and pork; continue cooking over medium heat, stirring occasionally, until pork is no longer pink (8 to 10 minutes).
- Stir in rice and beans. Continue cooking, stirring occasionally, until heated through (1 to 2 minutes). Stir in soy sauce.

TIP: For an easy side-dish, omit pork.

6 servings

NUTRITION FACTS (1 serving)
Calories 260 • Protein 13 g • Carbohydrate 41 g
Fat 4 g • Cholesterol 20 mg • Sodium 550 mg

Salads and Side Dishes

FUSILLI, PEPPERS AND MOZZARELLA SALAD

Preparation time: 20 minutes
Chilling time: 1 hour

PASTA

4 oz	uncooked dried fusilli (thin corkscrew *or* pasta twists)	115 g

DRESSING

¼ cup	chopped fresh basil leaves*	50 mL
¼ cup	olive oil	50 mL
¼ cup	white wine vinegar	50 mL
3 tbsp	lemon juice	45 mL
1 tsp	sugar	5 mL
½ tsp	salt	2 mL
½ tsp	pepper	2 mL

SALAD

1 cup	whole kernel corn, cooked, drained	250 mL
1	can (15 oz/425 g) garbanzo beans, rinsed, drained	1
1 cup	cubed mozzarella cheese, ½-inch (1 cm)	250 mL
½	medium cucumber, sliced ¼-inch (5 mm), quartered	½
½ cup	roasted red peppers cut into strips	125 mL

- Cook fusilli according to package directions. Drain; rinse with cold water. Set aside.
- In large bowl, combine all dressing ingredients; mix well.
- Add cooked fusilli and all salad ingredients to dressing; toss to coat well. Cover and refrigerate at least 1 hour to blend flavors.

** Substitute 1 tbsp (15 mL) dried basil leaves.*

6 servings

NUTRITION FACTS (1 serving)
Calories 310 • Protein 12 g • Carbohydrate 34 g
Fat 14 g • Cholesterol 10 mg • Sodium 450 mg

SALAD GREENS WITH RASPBERRY DRESSING

Preparation time: 10 minutes

1 cup	fresh *or* frozen raspberries, drained	250 mL
1 tbsp	red wine vinegar	15 mL
2 tbsp	olive *or* vegetable oil	30 mL
1 tbsp	sugar	15 mL
2 tsp	stone-ground mustard	10 mL
4 cups	mixed salad greens	1 L

- In medium bowl, mash raspberries with fork until smooth. Add vinegar; gradually add oil. Stir in sugar and mustard.
- Serve with salad greens.

TIP: Raspberry dressing can be made ahead of time and stored in a tightly-covered container.

6 servings

NUTRITION FACTS (1 serving)
Calories 70 • Protein 1 g • Carbohydrate 6 g
Fat 5 g • Cholesterol 0 mg • Sodium 30 mg

SPICY CUCUMBERS AND TOMATOES IN SOUR CREAM

Preparation time: 15 minutes
Chilling time: 30 minutes

1 cup	sour cream (fat free *or* light)	250 mL
⅛ to ¼ tsp	ground red pepper	0.5 to 1 mL
⅛ tsp	ground cumin	0.5 mL
¼ cup	sliced green onions	50 mL
2	medium tomatoes, seeded, chopped	2
½	medium cucumber, chopped	½
2 tbsp	chopped fresh cilantro, if desired	30 mL
	Salt	
	Pepper	

- In medium bowl, combine sour cream, ground red pepper and cumin; mix well.
- Add all remaining ingredients; stir gently to coat. Season with salt and pepper to taste. Cover and refrigerate 30 minutes.

6 servings

NUTRITION FACTS (1 serving)
Calories 45 • Protein 2 g • Carbohydrate 9 g
Fat 1 g • Cholesterol 4 mg • Sodium 50 mg

Italian Summer Sauté

Preparation time: 15 minutes
Cooking time: 6 minutes

¼ cup	butter	50 mL
8 oz	fresh mushrooms, sliced	225 g
1	medium zucchini, thinly sliced	1
1	small onion, cut into rings	1
1 tsp	Italian seasoning*	5 mL
½ tsp	finely chopped fresh garlic	2 mL
1	medium tomato, cut into 10 wedges	1
1 cup	shredded mozzarella cheese	250 mL

- In large skillet, melt butter until sizzling; add mushrooms, zucchini, onion, Italian seasoning and garlic. Cook over medium heat, stirring occasionally, until vegetables are crisply tender (4 to 5 minutes).
- Add tomato; sprinkle with cheese. Cover and continue cooking until vegetables are crisply tender and cheese is melted (2 to 3 minutes).

** Substitute ¼ tsp (1 mL) each dried oregano, marjoram and basil leaves, and ⅛ tsp (0.5 mL) rubbed sage.*

4 servings

NUTRITION FACTS (1 serving)
Calories 120 • Protein 6 g • Carbohydrate 6 g
Fat 8 g • Cholesterol 20 mg • Sodium 170 mg

Pasta in Fresh Herb Sauce

Preparation time: 20 minutes
Cooking time: 5 minutes

8 oz	uncooked dried linguine	225 g
¼ cup	butter	50 mL
½ tsp	finely chopped fresh garlic	2 mL
⅓ cup	chopped fresh parsley	75 mL
1½ tsp	chopped fresh oregano leaves*	7 mL
1 tbsp	lemon juice	15 mL
½ cup	freshly grated Parmesan cheese	125 mL

- In large saucepan, cook linguine according to package directions. Drain.
- In same saucepan, melt butter until sizzling; add garlic. Cook over medium heat until garlic is softened (3 to 4 minutes).
- Stir in cooked linguine and all remaining ingredients *except* Parmesan cheese. Continue cooking, stirring constantly, until heated through (2 to 3 minutes). Stir in Parmesan cheese.

** Substitute ½ tsp (2 mL) dried oregano leaves.*

4 servings

NUTRITION FACTS (1 serving)
Calories 370 • Protein 13 g • Carbohydrate 44 g
Fat 16 g • Cholesterol 40 mg • Sodium 360 mg

FLAVORFUL ROASTED VEGETABLES

Preparation time: 15 minutes
Baking time: 27 minutes

⅓ cup	butter	75 mL
1 tsp	dried basil leaves	5 mL
½ tsp	finely chopped fresh garlic	2 mL
¼ tsp	salt	1 mL
¼ tsp	pepper	1 mL
¼ tsp	dried thyme leaves	1 mL
3 cups	cauliflower florets	750 mL
2 cups	broccoli florets	500 mL
4	medium carrots, cut into julienne strips	4
2	small onions, quartered	2

- Heat oven to 400°F (200°C). In 13 x 9-inch (33 x 23 cm) baking pan, melt butter in oven (5 to 6 minutes). Stir in basil, garlic, salt, pepper and thyme. Add all remaining ingredients; toss to coat.
- Cover with aluminum foil; bake for 22 to 27 minutes or until vegetables are crisply tender.

6 servings

NUTRITION FACTS (1 serving)
Calories 140 • Protein 3 g • Carbohydrate 11 g
Fat 11 g • Cholesterol 30 mg • Sodium 230 mg

COUNTRY-STYLE POTATO SALAD

Preparation time: 30 minutes
Chilling time: 4 hours

4 cups	water	1 L
8 cups	quartered small new red potatoes	2 L
1 cup	mayonnaise	250 mL
¼ cup	stone-ground mustard	50 mL
1 tsp	coarsely ground pepper	5 mL
½ tsp	salt	2 mL
¼ cup	balsamic *or* red wine vinegar	50 mL
½ cup	coarsely chopped sweet pickle	125 mL
½ cup	chopped fresh parsley	125 mL
4	stalks celery, sliced ¼-inch (5 mm)	4
4	hard-cooked eggs, coarsely chopped	4
2	medium red onions, coarsely chopped	2

- In large saucepan, bring water to a full boil; add potatoes. Cook over medium-high heat until potatoes are tender (12 to 15 minutes). Rinse under cold water.
- Meanwhile, in small bowl, combine mayonnaise, mustard, pepper and salt. Set aside.
- In large bowl, place potatoes; drizzle with vinegar. Add mayonnaise mixture and all remaining ingredients; toss to coat.
- Cover and refrigerate at least 4 hours to blend flavors.

8 servings

NUTRITION FACTS (1 serving)
Calories 400 • Protein 8 g • Carbohydrate 38 g
Fat 25 g • Cholesterol 125 mg • Sodium 580 mg

Fiesta Rice and Vegetables

Preparation time: 5 minutes
Cooking time: 7 minutes

1½ cups	water	375 mL
1 tsp	onion salt	5 mL
1½ cups	uncooked instant rice	375 mL
1 cup	frozen peas and carrots	250 mL
⅓ cup	mild salsa	75 mL

- In medium saucepan, bring water and onion salt to a full boil. Stir in rice and vegetables. Remove from heat. Cover and let stand 5 minutes.
- Stir salsa into rice mixture. Cook over medium heat until liquid is absorbed and mixture is heated through (2 to 3 minutes).

6 servings

NUTRITION FACTS (1 serving)
Calories 110 • Protein 3 g • Carbohydrate 23 g
Fat 0 g • Cholesterol 0 mg • Sodium 240 mg

Marinated Bean Salad

Preparation time: 15 minutes
Chilling time: 2 hours

Dressing

⅓ cup	herbed vinegar *or* cider vinegar	75 mL
2 tbsp	sugar	30 mL
1 tbsp	chopped fresh parsley	15 mL
2 tbsp	olive *or* vegetable oil	30 mL
¼ tsp	pepper	1 mL

Salad

1 cup	julienne-cut red onion strips	250 mL
1 cup	julienne-cut red pepper strips	250 mL
1	can (15 oz/425 g) garbanzo beans, rinsed, drained	1
1	can (15½ oz/439 g) dark kidney beans, rinsed, drained	1
1	can (15½ oz/439 g) pinto beans, rinsed, drained	1
1	jar (10 oz/284 g) pepperoncini, drained, seeded, sliced	1

- In small bowl, stir together all dressing ingredients. Set aside.
- In large bowl, combine all salad ingredients. Add dressing; toss to coat. Cover and refrigerate, stirring every hour, at least 2 hours.

TIP: Be creative and use other types of beans: wax, green, cannellini, etc.

6 servings

NUTRITION FACTS (1 serving)
Calories 290 • Protein 11 g • Carbohydrate 48 g
Fat 6 g • Cholesterol 0 mg • Sodium 660 mg

GLAZED ORANGE CARROTS

Preparation time: 10 minutes
Cooking time: 14 minutes

10	medium carrots, cut into 1-inch (2.5 cm) pieces	10
3 tbsp	butter	45 mL
2 tbsp	orange juice	30 mL
1 tbsp	firmly packed brown sugar	15 mL
1 tsp	grated orange peel	5 mL
¼ tsp	ground ginger*	1 mL

- In medium saucepan, place carrots; add enough water to cover. Bring to a full boil. Cook over medium heat until carrots are crisply tender (10 to 12 minutes). Drain; return to pan.

- Add all remaining ingredients. Continue cooking, stirring occasionally, until heated through (4 to 7 minutes).

** Substitute 1 tsp (5 mL) chopped fresh gingerroot.*

8 servings

NUTRITION FACTS (1 serving)
Calories 70 • Protein 1 g • Carbohydrate 8 g
Fat 4.5 g • Cholesterol 10 mg • Sodium 85 mg

RANCH SKILLET POTATOES

Preparation time: 15 minutes
Cooking time: 16 minutes

¾ cup	light sour cream	175 mL
¼ cup	fat free skim milk	50 mL
¾ tsp	garlic salt	3 mL
4	slices turkey bacon *or* bacon	4
1	bag (24 oz/680 g) frozen diced potatoes with onions and peppers	1
1	can (11 oz/312 g) whole kernel corn with green and red peppers, drained	1
	Pepper	

- In small bowl, stir together sour cream, milk and garlic salt. Set aside.
- In large nonstick skillet, cook bacon over medium heat until crisp (6 to 8 minutes). Remove bacon from skillet; let cool slightly. Tear bacon into small pieces. Set aside.
- To same skillet, add potatoes. Cook over medium heat, stirring occasionally, until potatoes are browned and heated through (8 to 12 minutes). Stir in bacon and corn. Continue cooking until heated through (1 minute).
- Stir in sour cream mixture. Continue cooking, stirring constantly, until heated through (1 minute). Season with pepper to taste.

8 servings

NUTRITION FACTS (1 serving)
Calories 120 • Protein 4 g • Carbohydrate 22 g
Fat 2 g • Cholesterol 15 mg • Sodium 300 mg

MAKE-AHEAD MASHED POTATOES

Preparation time: 10 minutes
Cooking time: 20 minutes
Baking time: 40 minutes

2 lbs	**potatoes, peeled, cut into 1-inch (2.5 cm) pieces**	**900 g**
⅓ cup	**water**	**75 mL**
½ tsp	**salt**	**2 mL**
1 cup	**milk**	**250 mL**
⅓ cup	**sour cream (regular, light *or* fat free)**	**75 mL**
1½ tsp	**dry ranch salad dressing**	**7 mL**
2 tbsp	**Roasted Garlic Butter with Olive Oil***	**30 mL**

- In medium saucepan, combine potatoes, water and salt. Cook over high heat until water comes to a boil. Reduce heat to low. Cover and cook until potatoes are fork tender (15 to 18 minutes). Drain.
- With potato masher or electric mixer, mash potatoes, gradually adding *⅔ cup (175 mL)* milk. Stir in sour cream and dressing mix.
- Spread potatoes evenly into medium casserole. Pour remaining milk over potatoes. *Do not mix.* Dot with garlic butter. Cover and refrigerate 4 hours or overnight.
- *Heat oven to 400°F (200°C).* Bake uncovered for 20 minutes; stir. Continue baking until heated through (20 to 30 minutes).

** Substitute 2 tbsp (30 mL) butter and ¼ tsp (1 mL) garlic powder.*

6 servings

NUTRITION FACTS (1 serving)
Calories 160 • Protein 4 g • Carbohydrate 21 g
Fat 7 g • Cholesterol 15 mg • Sodium 260 mg

ALL-AMERICAN BACON, LETTUCE AND TOMATO SALAD

Preparation time: 10 minutes

2	**large tomatoes, cubed ½-inch (1 cm)**	**2**
8	**slices crisply cooked bacon, crumbled**	**8**
6 cups	**mixed salad greens**	**1.5 L**
¾ cup	**creamy-style ranch dressing***	**175 mL**
2 cups	**shredded white or yellow American cheese**	**500 mL**

- In large serving bowl, layer tomatoes, bacon, salad greens, dressing and cheese. Toss just before serving.

** Substitute ¾ cup (175 mL) of your favorite creamy-style dressing.*

8 servings

NUTRITION FACTS (1 serving)
Calories 240 • Protein 10 g • Carbohydrate 4 g
Fat 21 g • Cholesterol 40 mg • Sodium 610 mg

STRAWBERRY 'N POPPY SEED SALAD

Preparation time: 25 minutes
Chilling time: 30 minutes

DRESSING

½ cup	sour cream (regular, light *or* fat free)	125 mL
1 tbsp	sugar	15 mL
1 tsp	poppy seeds	5 mL
1 tsp	grated orange peel	5 mL
2 to 3 tbsp	milk	30 to 45 mL
1 tbsp	orange juice	15 mL

SALAD

¼ cup	coarsely chopped pecans	50 mL
2 tbsp	sugar	30 mL
3 cups	torn lettuce	750 mL
3 cups	spinach leaves, washed, trimmed	750 mL
2 cups	sliced fresh strawberries	500 mL

- In small bowl, stir together all dressing ingredients. Cover and refrigerate at least 30 minutes.
- In medium skillet, combine pecans and sugar. Cook over medium heat, stirring constantly, until sugar is melted and pecans are coated and lightly browned (5 to 8 minutes). Spread on waxed paper; let cool completely.
- Just before serving, in large bowl, toss together pecans and all remaining salad ingredients. Serve with dressing.

6 servings

NUTRITION FACTS (1 serving)
Calories 120 • Protein 4 g • Carbohydrate 18 g
Fat 5 g • Cholesterol 3 mg • Sodium 50 mg

THAI PEANUT SLAW

Preparation time: 20 minutes

SALAD

4 cups	coleslaw mix *or* shredded cabbage	1 L
½ cup	coarsely chopped cucumber	125 mL
⅓ cup	sliced green onions	75 mL
¼ cup	salted peanuts	50 mL
¼ cup	finely chopped red pepper	50 mL

DRESSING

½ cup	salted peanuts, very finely ground	125 mL
3 tbsp	peanut or vegetable oil	45 mL
3 tbsp	rice vinegar or vinegar	45 mL
1 tbsp	soy sauce	15 mL
1½ tsp	sugar	7 mL
1 tsp	finely chopped fresh garlic	5 mL
¼ tsp	red pepper flakes	1 mL

- In large bowl, combine all salad ingredients.
- In small bowl, stir together all dressing ingredients. Just before serving, pour dressing over salad; toss to coat.

8 servings

NUTRITION FACTS (1 serving)
Calories 120 • Protein 3 g • Carbohydrate 6 g
Fat 10 g • Cholesterol 0 mg • Sodium 220 mg

Strawberry 'n Poppy Seed Salad

Cheddar Rice Florentine

***Preparation time:* 20 minutes**
***Baking time:* 30 minutes**

Topping

¼ cup	dried bread crumbs	50 mL
¼ cup	slivered blanched almonds	50 mL
2 tbsp	chopped fresh parsley	30 mL
2 tbsp	butter, melted	30 mL

Sauce

1 cup	shredded Cheddar cheese	250 mL
½ cup	milk	125 mL
1	can (10¾ oz/318 mL) condensed cream of celery soup	1
1	can (4 oz/113 g) mushroom stems and pieces, drained	1
1	stalk celery, diagonally sliced ⅛-inch (3 mm)	1
1 tbsp	instant minced onion	15 mL
½ tsp	salt	2 mL

Spinach and Rice

1	package (10 oz/284 g) frozen chopped spinach, thawed, well-drained	1
1½ cups	cooked brown *or* long grain rice	375 mL

- Heat oven to 350°F (180°C). In small bowl, stir together all topping ingredients. Set aside.
- In medium bowl, stir together all sauce ingredients.
- Place spinach in bottom of medium casserole. Layer *¾ cup (175 mL)* sauce and *¾ cup (175 mL)* rice over spinach; repeat layers. Top with remaining sauce; sprinkle with topping.
- Bake for 30 to 40 minutes or until bubbly around edges.

6 servings

NUTRITION FACTS (1 serving)
Calories 280 • Protein 11 g • Carbohydrate 24 g
Fat 16 g • Cholesterol 40 mg • Sodium 880 mg

1

In small bowl, stir together all topping ingredients.

2

In medium bowl, stir together all sauce ingredients.

3

Place spinach in bottom of medium casserole. Layer ¾ cup (175 mL) sauce over spinach.

Layer ¾ cup (175 mL) rice over sauce; repeat layers.

Top with remaining sauce; sprinkle with topping.

HARVEST BAKE

Preparation time: 15 minutes
Baking time: 35 minutes

POTATOES

¼ cup	butter	50 mL
¼ cup	firmly packed brown sugar	50 mL
1	can (23 oz/652 g) sweet potatoes *or* yams, drained	1
2 tbsp	apple juice	30 mL

TOPPING

¼ cup	firmly packed brown sugar	50 mL
1 tbsp	all-purpose flour	15 mL
¼ tsp	ground cardamom	1 mL
1 tbsp	cold butter	15 mL
2 tbsp	chopped pecans	30 mL
1	medium apple, cored, thinly sliced	1

- Heat oven to 350°F (180°C). In medium casserole, melt ¼ cup (50 mL) butter in oven (5 minutes). Stir in brown sugar. Add sweet potatoes and apple juice. Mash with potato masher or electric mixer until smooth.
- In small bowl, combine ¼ cup (50 mL) brown sugar, flour and cardamom; cut in 1 tbsp (15 mL) butter until crumbly. Stir in pecans. Sprinkle *half* of mixture over potatoes. Arrange apple slices on top; sprinkle with remaining mixture.
- Bake for 35 to 40 minutes or until apples are crisply tender and potatoes are thoroughly heated.

6 servings

NUTRITION FACTS (1 serving)
Calories 290 • Protein 2 g • Carbohydrate 46 g
Fat 12 g • Cholesterol 25 mg • Sodium 160 mg

CREAMY MUSTARD COLESLAW

Preparation time: 30 minutes
Chilling time: 1 hour

COLESLAW

5 cups	finely shredded cabbage	1.25 L
¼ cup	finely chopped celery	50 mL
¼ cup	finely chopped green pepper	50 mL
2 tbsp	finely chopped radishes	30 mL
1 tbsp	chopped green onions	15 mL

DRESSING

⅓ cup	mayonnaise	75 mL
¼ cup	sour cream (regular, light *or* fat free)	50 mL
1 tbsp	sugar	15 mL
1 tbsp	prepared mustard	15 mL
1 tbsp	vinegar	15 mL
½ tsp	dried dill weed	2 mL
¼ tsp	salt	1 mL

- In large bowl, combine all coleslaw ingredients.
- In small bowl, stir together all dressing ingredients. Pour dressing over coleslaw; toss well to coat. Cover and refrigerate at least 1 hour.

8 servings

NUTRITION FACTS (1 serving)
Calories 100 • Protein 1 g • Carbohydrate 5 g
Fat 9 g • Cholesterol 10 mg • Sodium 160 mg

SPINACH SALAD WITH HERB DRESSING

Preparation time: 20 minutes
Chilling time: 2 hours

DRESSING

½ cup	sour cream	125 mL
¼ cup	mayonnaise	50 mL
¼ cup	milk	50 mL
2 tsp	chopped green onions	10 mL
1 tsp	prepared mustard	5 mL
¼ tsp	dried basil leaves	1 mL
⅛ tsp	garlic salt	0.5 mL

SALAD

4 cups	torn spinach leaves	1 L
1 cup	sliced fresh mushrooms	250 mL
1 cup	halved cherry tomatoes	250 mL

- In small bowl, stir together all dressing ingredients. Cover and refrigerate at least 2 hours.
- In large bowl, toss together all salad ingredients. Serve with dressing.

6 servings

NUTRITION FACTS (1 serving)
Calories 130 • Protein 3 g • Carbohydrate 5 g
Fat 12 g • Cholesterol 15 mg • Sodium 150 mg

QUICK JALAPEÑO POTATO SALAD

Preparation time: 10 minutes
Chilling time: 30 minutes

1 pint	deli potato salad	500 mL
¼ cup	chopped red peppers	50 mL
2 tbsp	bottled sliced jalapeño peppers	30 mL
2 tbsp	chopped fresh cilantro	30 mL

- In medium bowl, combine all ingredients; mix well.
- Cover and refrigerate 30 minutes, or until serving time.
- Spoon into serving bowl lined with lettuce, if desired.

4 servings

NUTRITION FACTS (1 serving)
Calories 140 • Protein 2 g • Carbohydrate 17 g
Fat 7 g • Cholesterol 5 mg • Sodium 400 mg

CREAMY FRUIT SALAD

Preparation time: 10 minutes
Chilling time: 2 hours

¾ cup	sour cream (regular, light *or* fat free)	175 mL
½ cup	miniature marshmallows	125 mL
½ cup	flaked coconut	125 mL
1	can (15 oz/425 g) fruit cocktail, drained	1
1 tsp	grated lemon *or* orange peel	5 mL
	Fresh mint leaves, if desired	

- In medium bowl, combine all ingredients; mix well. Cover and chill at least 2 hours. Garnish with fresh mint leaves, if desired.

4 servings

NUTRITION FACTS (1 serving)
Calories 240 • Protein 3 g • Carbohydrate 31 g
Fat 13 g • Cholesterol 25 mg • Sodium 9 mg

EASY STRAWBERRY ORANGE SALAD

Preparation time: 15 minutes
Chilling time: 4 hours

2	packages (3 oz/85 g each) strawberry-flavored gelatin	2
2 cups	boiling water	500 mL
1	package (10 oz/284 g) frozen lightly sweetened strawberries, thawed, drained, *juice reserved*	1
⅓ cup	orange juice	75 mL
1	can (11 oz/312 g) mandarin orange segments, drained	1
⅓ cup	sour cream (regular, light *or* fat free)	75 mL

- In large bowl, place gelatin. Add boiling water; stir until gelatin is dissolved.
- In small bowl, combine reserved strawberry juice and orange juice; stir into gelatin. *Set aside 1 tbsp (15 mL) gelatin mixture.*
- Cover gelatin mixture and refrigerate until slightly thickened (1 to 2 hours). Gently stir in strawberries and orange segments. If desired, pour into gelatin mold. Cover and refrigerate until set (3 to 4 hours).
- Meanwhile, in small bowl, stir together sour cream and reserved strawberry gelatin mixture until well mixed. Cover and refrigerate until serving time.
- Serve sour cream mixture with salad.

8 servings

NUTRITION FACTS (1 serving)
Calories 90 • Protein 1 g • Carbohydrate 17 g
Fat 2 g • Cholesterol 5 mg • Sodium 20 mg

Creamy Fruit Salad

Desserts

Warm Pear Crisp

Preparation time: 20 minutes
Baking time: 40 minutes

Filling

4	medium pears, peeled, cored, sliced ½-inch (1 cm)	4
1 tbsp	lemon juice	15 mL
1 tsp	cinnamon	5 mL
¼ tsp	ground nutmeg	1 mL

Topping

½ cup	all-purpose flour	125 mL
½ cup	quick-cooking oats	125 mL
½ cup	firmly packed brown sugar	125 mL
⅓ cup	butter, softened	75 mL

- Heat oven to 375°F (190°C). Place pears in 9-inch (23 cm) square baking pan. Sprinkle with lemon juice, cinnamon and nutmeg.
- In small mixer bowl, combine flour, oats, brown sugar and butter. Beat at low speed, scraping bowl often, until crumbly (1 to 2 minutes). Sprinkle evenly over pears.
- Bake for 40 to 50 minutes or until pears are fork tender and top is golden brown. Serve warm with ice cream or sweetened whipped cream, if desired.

6 servings

NUTRITION FACTS (1 serving)
Calories 430 • Protein 5 g • Carbohydrate 63 g
Fat 19 g • Cholesterol 60 mg • Sodium 170 mg

GINGERBREAD WEDGES WITH CIDER SAUCE

Preparation time: 20 minutes
Baking time: 30 minutes

GINGERBREAD

1¾ cups	all-purpose flour	425 mL
⅓ cup	firmly packed brown sugar	75 mL
½ cup	butter, softened	125 mL
½ cup	light molasses	125 mL
½ cup	buttermilk*	125 mL
1	egg	1
1 tsp	baking soda	5 mL
½ tsp	ground ginger	2 mL
¼ tsp	ground cloves	1 mL
¼ tsp	ground nutmeg	1 mL

CIDER SAUCE

1 cup	apple cider	250 mL
⅓ cup	firmly packed brown sugar	75 mL
1 tbsp	butter	15 mL
1 tbsp	lemon juice	15 mL
⅛ tsp	ground cloves	0.5 mL
1 tbsp	cornstarch	15 mL
1 tbsp	water	15 mL

- Heat oven to 350°F (180°C). In large mixer bowl, combine all gingerbread ingredients. Beat at low speed, scraping bowl often, until well mixed (2 to 3 minutes).
- Pour batter into greased and floured 9-inch (23 cm) round cake pan. Bake for 30 to 40 minutes or until top springs back when touched lightly in center. Let cool 10 minutes. Remove from pan.
- Meanwhile, in small saucepan, combine all cider sauce ingredients *except* cornstarch and water. Cook over medium heat, stirring occasionally, until mixture comes to a full boil (7 to 10 minutes). Boil 3 minutes.
- In small bowl, combine cornstarch and water. Stir into hot cider sauce mixture. Continue cooking, stirring constantly, until sauce is thickened (1 to 2 minutes). Serve warm over gingerbread.

9 servings

** Substitute 1½ tsp (7 mL) vinegar plus enough milk to equal ½ cup (125 mL).*

NUTRITION FACTS (1 serving)
Calories 320 • Protein 4 g • Carbohydrate 50 g
Fat 13 g • Cholesterol 55 mg • Sodium 410 mg

SOUR CREAM POUND CAKE

***Preparation time:* 30 minutes**
***Baking time:* 50 minutes**

1 cup	**sugar**	**250 mL**
1 cup	**butter, softened**	**250 mL**
1 cup	**sour cream (regular, light *or* fat free)**	**250 mL**
3	**eggs**	**3**
½ tsp	**vanilla**	**2 mL**
2 cups	**all-purpose flour**	**500 mL**
1 tsp	**baking powder**	**5 mL**
1 tsp	**baking soda**	**5 mL**
½ tsp	**salt**	**2 mL**

- Heat oven to 350°F (180°C). In large mixer bowl, beat sugar and butter at medium speed, scraping bowl often, until creamy (2 to 3 minutes). Add sour cream, eggs and vanilla; continue beating until well mixed.
- Reduce speed to low; add all remaining ingredients. Beat, scraping bowl often, until smooth (1 to 2 minutes).
- Spoon batter into large greased and floured Bundt® pan. Bake for 50 to 60 minutes or until toothpick inserted in center comes out clean. Let cool in pan 5 minutes. Remove from pan; let cool completely.

12 servings

NUTRITION FACTS (1 serving)
Calories 335 • Protein 5 g • Carbohydrate 33 g
Fat 21 g • Cholesterol 105 mg • Sodium 430 mg

1

In large mixer bowl, beat sugar and butter at medium speed, scraping bowl often, until creamy.

2

Add sour cream, eggs and vanilla; continue beating until well mixed.

3

Add all remaining ingredients. Beat, scraping bowl often, until smooth.

Spoon batter into large greased and floured Bundt® pan.

Bake for 50 to 60 minutes. Let cool in pan 5 minutes.

Remove from pan; let cool completely.

Vanilla Crazy Cake

Preparation time: 15 minutes
Baking time: 30 minutes

1¼ cups	all-purpose flour	300 mL
1 cup	sugar	250 mL
1½ tsp	baking powder	7 mL
½ tsp	salt	2 mL
1	egg	1
1 tsp	vanilla	5 mL
⅓ cup	vegetable oil	75 mL
¾ cup	milk	175 mL
¼ cup	chopped pecans	50 mL
½ cup	semi-sweet real chocolate chips	125 mL

- Heat oven to 350°F (180°C). In 8-inch (20 cm) square baking pan, combine flour, sugar, baking powder and salt. Set aside.
- In small bowl, with wire whisk, stir together egg and vanilla. Make 2 indentations in flour mixture; pour oil in one and egg mixture in the other. Pour milk over flour mixture; mix well. Stir in pecans.
- Bake for 30 to 40 minutes or until toothpick inserted in center comes out clean. Sprinkle chocolate chips on warm cake. Let stand 2 minutes; slightly swirl melted chips.

9 servings

NUTRITION FACTS (1 serving)
Calories 310 • Protein 4 g • Carbohydrate 43 g
Fat 14 g • Cholesterol 25 mg • Sodium 220 mg

Peach pie

Preparation time: 20 minutes
Baking time: 55 minutes

1	**purchased 9-inch (23 cm) double pie crust**	**1**
1 cup	**sugar**	**250 mL**
2 tbsp	**cornstarch**	**30 mL**
2	**bags (16 oz/454 g each) frozen sliced peaches, thawed, drained***	**2**
1 tbsp	**lemon juice**	**15 mL**
½ tsp	**vanilla**	**2 mL**
1 tbsp	**butter, melted**	**15 mL**
1 tsp	**sugar**	**5 mL**

- Heat oven to 400°F (200°C). Prepare pie crust as directed on package.
- In large bowl, combine sugar and cornstarch. Add peaches, lemon juice and vanilla; toss lightly to coat. Spoon into prepared crust.
- Place top crust over peaches. Crimp or flute edge; cut 8 large slits in top crust. Brush with melted butter; sprinkle with 1 tsp (5 mL) sugar. Cover edge of pastry with 2-inch (5 cm) strip of aluminum foil.
- Bake for 35 minutes. Remove aluminum foil. Continue baking for 20 to 25 minutes or until crust is lightly browned and juice begins to bubble. Serve warm or cool.

** Substitute 6 ripe medium peaches, peeled, pitted, sliced ¼-inch (5 mm).*

8 servings

NUTRITION FACTS (1 serving)
Calories 400 • Protein 4 g • Carbohydrate 59 g
Fat 17 g • Cholesterol 45 mg • Sodium 240 mg

ROCKY ROAD CHOCOLATE CAKE

Preparation time: 20 minutes
Baking time: 32 minutes

CAKE

2 cups	all-purpose flour	500 mL
1½ cups	sugar	375 mL
1 cup	water	250 mL
½ cup	unsweetened cocoa	125 mL
½ cup	butter, softened	125 mL
3	eggs	3
1¼ tsp	baking powder	6 mL
1 tsp	baking soda	5 mL
1 tsp	vanilla	5 mL

FROSTING

2 cups	miniature marshmallows	500 mL
¼ cup	butter	50 mL
1	package (3 oz/85 g) cream cheese	1
1	square (1 oz/28 g) unsweetened chocolate	1
2 tbsp	milk	30 mL
3 cups	powdered sugar	750 mL
1 tsp	vanilla	5 mL
½ cup	coarsely chopped salted peanuts	125 mL

- Heat oven to 350°F (180°C). In large mixer bowl, combine all cake ingredients. Beat at low speed, scraping bowl often, until all ingredients are moistened. Increase speed to high. Beat, scraping bowl often, until smooth (1 to 2 minutes).
- Pour batter into greased and floured 13 x 9-inch (33 x 23 cm) baking pan. Bake for 30 to 40 minutes or until toothpick inserted in center comes out clean. Sprinkle with marshmallows. Continue baking 2 minutes or until marshmallows are softened.
- Meanwhile, in medium saucepan, combine ¼ cup (50 mL) butter, cream cheese, chocolate and milk. Cook over medium heat, stirring occasionally, until melted (8 to 10 minutes).
- Remove from heat; stir in powdered sugar and vanilla until smooth. Pour over marshmallows and swirl together. Sprinkle with peanuts.

15 servings

NUTRITION FACTS (1 serving)
Calories 400 • Protein 6 g • Carbohydrate 61 g
Fat 16 g • Cholesterol 75 mg • Sodium 290 mg

ICE CREAM FILLED CHOCOLATE CUPS

Preparation time: 30 minutes
Chilling time: 30 minutes

¼ cup	butter	50 mL
2	squares (1 oz/28 g each) semi-sweet baking chocolate	2
1	jar (7 oz/207 mL) marshmallow crème	1
4 cups	crispy rice cereal	1 L
½ gallon	cookies and cream ice cream	2 L

- In medium saucepan, combine butter and chocolate. Cook over low heat, stirring constantly, until melted (4 to 6 minutes). Stir in marshmallow crème until well mixed.
- In large bowl, combine cereal and marshmallow crème mixture; mix well. With well-buttered fingers, press about *¼ cup (50 mL)* cereal mixture onto bottom and sides of each cup of 12-cup greased muffin pan. Refrigerate at least 30 minutes or until set.
- Just before serving, remove chocolate cups from pan. Place *1 large scoop* ice cream into each cup.

TIP: If only 6 cups are needed, press remaining mixture into greased 8-inch (20 cm) square baking pan; cut into squares. Store refrigerated. Do not freeze.

12 servings

NUTRITION FACTS (1 serving)
Calories 370 • Protein 4 g • Carbohydrate 52 g
Fat 18 g • Cholesterol 50 mg • Sodium 260 mg

MOCHA ALMOND BARS

Preparation time: 20 minutes
Baking time: 25 minutes

BARS

2¼ cups	all-purpose flour	550 mL
1 cup	sugar	250 mL
1 cup	butter, softened	250 mL
1	egg	1
1 tsp	instant coffee granules	5 mL
1 cup	sliced almonds	250 mL

GLAZE

¾ cup	powdered sugar	175 mL
¼ tsp	almond extract	1 mL
1 to 2 tbsp	milk	15 to 30 mL

- Heat oven to 350°F (180°C). In small mixer bowl, combine all bars ingredients *except* almonds. Beat at low speed, scraping bowl often, until well mixed (2 to 3 minutes). By hand, stir in almonds.
- Press onto bottom of greased 13 x 9-inch (33 x 23 cm) baking pan. Bake for 25 to 30 minutes or until edges are lightly browned.
- Meanwhile, in small bowl, stir together powdered sugar, almond extract and enough milk for desired glazing consistency. Drizzle glaze over warm bars. Let cool completely; cut into bars.

3 dozen

NUTRITION FACTS (1 bar)
Calories 120 • Protein 2 g • Carbohydrate 14 g
Fat 7 g • Cholesterol 20 mg • Sodium 55 mg

OLD-FASHIONED BREAD PUDDING

Preparation time: 15 minutes
Baking time: 40 minutes

PUDDING

8	slices white bread, cubed	8
½ cup	raisins	125 mL
2 cups	milk	500 mL
¼ cup	butter	50 mL
½ cup	sugar	125 mL
2	eggs, slightly beaten	2
1 tsp	vanilla	5 mL
½ tsp	ground nutmeg	2 mL

SAUCE

½ cup	butter	125 mL
½ cup	sugar	125 mL
½ cup	firmly packed brown sugar	125 mL
½ cup	whipping cream	125 mL
1 tsp	vanilla	5 mL

- Heat oven to 350°F (180°C). In large bowl, combine bread and raisins. In small saucepan, combine milk and ¼ cup (50 mL) butter; cook over medium heat until melted. Pour over bread; let stand 10 minutes. Stir in remaining pudding ingredients. Pour into greased 1½ quart (1½ L) casserole. Bake for 40 to 50 minutes or until set in center.

- In small saucepan, combine all sauce ingredients *except* vanilla. Cook over medium heat, stirring occasionally, until mixture thickens and comes to a full boil (5 to 8 minutes). Stir in vanilla. Serve warm pudding with sauce. Store refrigerated.

8 servings

NUTRITION FACTS (1 serving)
Calories 470 • Protein 6 g • Carbohydrate 56 g
Fat 26 g • Cholesterol 125 mg • Sodium 310 mg

GLISTENING RASPBERRY BARS

Preparation time: 15 minutes
Baking time: 18 minutes

CRUST

1¼ cups	all-purpose flour	300 mL
⅓ cup	sugar	75 mL
½ cup	butter, softened	125 mL

TOPPING

¼ cup	honey	50 mL
2 tbsp	butter	30 mL
½ cup	quick-cooking oats	125 mL
¼ cup	sliced almonds	50 mL
¼ cup	flaked coconut	50 mL

FILLING

1 cup	raspberry preserves	250 mL

- Heat oven to 350°F (180°C). In small mixer bowl, combine all crust ingredients. Beat at low speed, scraping bowl often, until mixture is crumbly (1 to 2 minutes).
- Press onto bottom of greased 9-inch (23 cm) square baking pan. Bake 18 to 23 minutes, or until edges are lightly browned.
- Meanwhile, in medium saucepan, combine honey and butter. Cook over medium heat, stirring constantly, until butter is melted (1 to 2 minutes). Stir in all remaining topping ingredients.
- Spread preserves over hot partially baked crust; spoon topping mixture over filling. Continue baking for 15 to 20 minutes or until edges are lightly browned. Let cool completely; cut into bars.

18 bars

NUTRITION FACTS (1 bar)
Calories 180 • Protein 2 g • Carbohydrate 28 g
Fat 8 g • Cholesterol 20 mg • Sodium 80 mg

Baked Lemon Pudding Soufflé

Preparation time: 20 minutes
Baking time: 45 minutes

3	**eggs, separated**	**3**
1 cup	**sugar**	**250 mL**
⅓ cup	**butter, softened**	**75 mL**
¼ cup	**lemon juice**	**50 mL**
1 tbsp	**grated lemon peel**	**15 mL**
¼ cup	**all-purpose flour**	**50 mL**
⅛ tsp	**salt**	**0.5 mL**
1 cup	**milk**	**250 mL**
	Powdered sugar, if desired	

- Heat oven to 350°F (180°C). In small mixer bowl, beat egg whites at medium speed until foamy (1 to 2 minutes). Beat at high speed, gradually adding *¼ cup (50 mL)* sugar, until stiff and glossy (2 to 3 minutes); set aside.
- In large mixer bowl, combine remaining sugar and butter. Beat at medium speed, scraping bowl often, until creamy (1 to 2 minutes). Add egg yolks, lemon juice and peel. Continue beating, scraping bowl often, until well mixed (1 minute).
- Add flour and salt. Continue beating, scraping bowl often, until well mixed (1 minute). By hand, stir in milk. Gently stir in beaten egg whites.
- Pour mixture into soufflé dish or medium casserole. Place dish in 9-inch (23 cm) square baking pan. Place baking pan on oven rack; pour boiling water into baking pan to ½-inch (1 cm) depth.
- Bake for 45 to 55 minutes or until golden brown. Remove soufflé dish from water; let cool 10 minutes. Sprinkle with powdered sugar, if desired.

6 servings

NUTRITION FACTS (1 serving)
Calories 300 • Protein 5 g • Carbohydrate 41 g
Fat 14 g • Cholesterol 140 mg • Sodium 200 mg

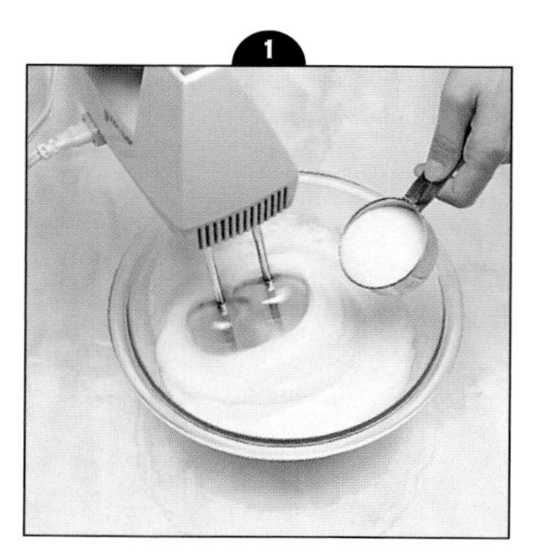

1 *Beat egg whites at high speed, gradually adding ¼ cup (50 mL) sugar, until stiff and glossy.*

2 *In large mixer bowl, combine remaining sugar and butter. Add egg yolks, lemon juice and peel.*

3 *Add flour and salt. Continue beating, scraping bowl often, until well mixed.*

By hand, stir in milk.

Gently stir in beaten egg whites.

Pour mixture into soufflé dish or medium casserole.

CHUNKY PEANUT BUTTER SWIRL BARS

Preparation time: 15 minutes
Baking time: 25 minutes

½ cup	sugar	125 mL
½ cup	firmly packed brown sugar	125 mL
½ cup	butter, softened	125 mL
½ cup	chunky peanut butter	125 mL
2	eggs	2
1 tsp	vanilla	5 mL
1½ cups	all-purpose flour	375 mL
½ tsp	baking soda	2 mL
¼ tsp	salt	1 mL
1	bag (8 oz/225 g) chocolate-covered peanut butter-flavored round candies*	1
½ cup	chopped peanuts	125 mL
1 cup	semi-sweet real chocolate chips	250 mL

- Heat oven to 350°F (180°C). In large mixer bowl, combine sugar, brown sugar, butter, peanut butter, eggs and vanilla. Beat at medium speed, scraping bowl often, until well mixed (1 to 2 minutes). Reduce speed to low; add flour, baking soda and salt. Beat until well mixed (1 to 2 minutes). By hand, stir in candies and peanuts.

- Spread batter into greased 13 x 9-inch (33 x 23 cm) baking pan. Bake for 25 to 30 minutes or until golden brown. Sprinkle with chocolate chips; let stand 5 minutes. Spread melted chips over bars. Let cool completely; cut into bars.

48 bars

** Substitute three 2.1-oz (60 g) chocolate-covered peanut butter-flavored bars.*

NUTRITION FACTS (1 bar)
Calories 150 • Protein 3 g • Carbohydrate 18 g
Fat 8 g • Cholesterol 20 mg • Sodium 100 mg

Cherry Custard Clafouti

Preparation time: 10 minutes
Baking time: 40 minutes

1	**can (16 oz/454 g) Bing cherries, well-drained**	**1**
2 tbsp	**sugar**	**30 mL**
1 cup	**milk**	**250 mL**
½ cup	**all-purpose flour**	**125 mL**
½ cup	**sugar**	**125 mL**
3	**eggs**	**3**
1 tsp	**vanilla**	**5 mL**
½ tsp	**almond extract**	**2 mL**
2 tbsp	**powdered sugar**	**30 mL**

- Heat oven to 350°F (180°C). Place cherries in greased 9-inch (23 cm) pie pan; sprinkle with 2 tbsp (30 mL) sugar.
- In blender container, place milk; add all remaining ingredients *except* powdered sugar. Cover and blend at medium speed until smooth (1 to 2 minutes). Pour over cherries.
- Bake for 40 to 50 minutes or until knife inserted in center comes out clean. Sprinkle with powdered sugar. Store refrigerated.

8 servings

NUTRITION FACTS (1 serving)
Calories 160 • Protein 5 g • Carbohydrate 31 g
Fat 3 g • Cholesterol 80 mg • Sodium 55 mg

Frozen Strawberry Margarita Pie

Preparation time: 30 minutes
Baking time: 8 minutes
Chilling time: 45 minutes
Freezing time: 6 hours
Standing time: 20 minutes

Crust

1 cup	**finely crushed pretzels**	**250 mL**
⅓ cup	**butter, melted**	**75 mL**
3 tbsp	**sugar**	**45 mL**

Filling

2	**envelopes (¼ oz/7 g each) unflavored gelatin**	**2**
½ cup	**water**	**125 mL**
3 cups	**strawberries, hulled, *4 reserved***	**750 mL**
1 cup	**lowfat strawberry yogurt**	**250 mL**
½ cup	**sugar**	**125 mL**
¼ cup	**tequila *or* orange juice**	**50 mL**
1	**can (6 oz/170 g) frozen limeade concentrate, slightly thawed**	**1**
1 cup	**frozen whipped topping, thawed**	**250 mL**
8	**small pretzels**	**8**

- Heat oven to 350°F (180°C). In medium bowl, stir together all crust ingredients. Press onto bottom and sides of 9-inch (23 cm) pie pan. Bake for 8 to 10 minutes or until lightly browned. Let cool completely.
- Meanwhile, in small saucepan, sprinkle gelatin over water; let stand 5 minutes to soften. Cook over medium heat until gelatin is dissolved (1 to 2 minutes).
- In food processor bowl or blender container, place strawberries. Cover and process on high speed until well mixed (1 minute). Add gelatin mixture, yogurt, sugar, tequila and limeade. Continue processing until well mixed. Cover and refrigerate until mixture mounds when dropped from a spoon (45 to 60 minutes).
- Spoon into prepared crust. Freeze until firm (6 hours or overnight).
- Slice 4 reserved strawberries. Garnish pie with strawberry slices, whipped topping and pretzels. Let stand at room temperature 20 to 30 minutes before serving.

8 servings

NUTRITION FACTS (1 serving)
Calories 280 • Protein 4 g • Carbohydrate 46 g
Fat 8 g • Cholesterol 15 mg • Sodium 280 mg

DIXIE'S FRESH APPLE CAKE

Preparation time: 30 minutes
Baking time: 40 minutes

CAKE

3 cups	all-purpose flour	750 mL
2 tsp	baking soda	10 mL
1 tsp	baking powder	5 mL
1 tsp	cinnamon	5 mL
½ tsp	salt	2 mL
½ tsp	ground nutmeg	2 mL
¼ tsp	ground cloves	1 mL
2 cups	firmly packed brown sugar	500 mL
1 cup	butter	250 mL
2	eggs	2
1 cup	cold brewed coffee	250 mL
1 cup	raisins	250 mL
1 cup	chopped walnuts	250 mL
2	tart medium apples, peeled, cored, coarsely chopped	2

TOPPING

½ cup	sugar	125 mL
¼ cup	firmly packed brown sugar	50 mL
½ tsp	cinnamon	2 mL
½ cup	chopped walnuts	125 mL

- Heat oven to 350°F (180°C). In medium bowl, combine flour, baking soda, baking powder, 1 tsp (5 mL) cinnamon, salt, nutmeg and cloves; set aside.
- In large mixer bowl, combine 2 cups (500 mL) brown sugar and butter. Beat at medium speed, scraping bowl often, until creamy (2 to 3 minutes). Continue beating, adding eggs one at a time, beating well after each addition (1 to 2 minutes).
- Reduce speed to low. Beat, adding flour mixture alternately with coffee, until well mixed (1 to 2 minutes). By hand, stir in raisins, 1 cup (250 mL) walnuts and apples.
- Spread batter into greased 13 x 9-inch (33 x 23 cm) baking pan. In medium bowl, combine all topping ingredients. Sprinkle over batter; gently press into batter. Bake for 40 to 50 minutes or until toothpick inserted in center comes out clean.

20 servings

NUTRITION FACTS (1 serving)
Calories 360 • Protein 4 g • Carbohydrate 53 g
Fat 16 g • Cholesterol 45 mg • Sodium 290 mg

German Chocolate Cheesecake Pie

Preparation time: 30 minutes
Baking time: 25 minutes
Chilling time: 2 hours

Crust

1 cup	chopped toasted slivered almonds	250 mL
1 cup	flaked coconut	250 mL
⅓ cup	butter, melted	75 mL
⅓ cup	sugar	75 mL

Filling

½ cup	sugar	125 mL
2	packages (8 oz/225 g each) cream cheese, softened	2
2	eggs	2
1	bar (4 oz/115 g) sweet chocolate, melted	1

- Heat oven to 350°F (180°C). In medium bowl, stir together all crust ingredients; *reserve ⅓ cup (75 mL) for topping*. Press remaining crust mixture onto bottom and halfway up sides of 9-inch (23 cm) pie pan; set aside.
- In large mixer bowl, combine ½ cup (125 mL) sugar and cream cheese. Beat at medium speed, scraping bowl often, until creamy (1 to 2 minutes). Add eggs. Continue beating, scraping bowl often, until well mixed (1 to 2 minutes). Add chocolate. Continue beating, scraping bowl often, until well mixed (1 to 2 minutes).
- Pour chocolate mixture into prepared pie crust. Bake for 25 to 35 minutes or until center is just set. Let cool; sprinkle with reserved crust mixture. Refrigerate at least 2 hours.

8 servings

NUTRITION FACTS (1 serving)
Calories 580 • Protein 10 g • Carbohydrate 38 g
Fat 45 g • Cholesterol 135 mg • Sodium 270 mg

1

Press crust mixture onto bottom and halfway up sides of pie pan, reserving ⅓ cup (75 mL) for topping.

2

In large mixer bowl, combine ½ cup (125 mL) sugar and cream cheese. Beat at medium speed, scraping bowl often, until creamy.

3

Add eggs. Continue beating, scraping bowl often, until well mixed.

Add chocolate.

Beat chocolate into egg mixture, scraping bowl often, until well mixed.

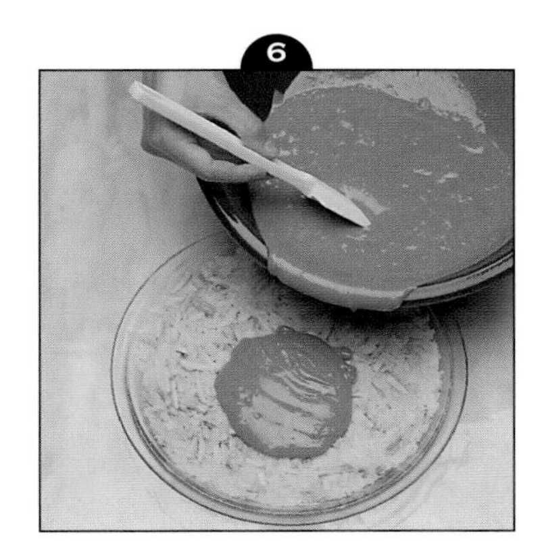

Pour chocolate mixture into prepared pie crust.

CARAMEL SALTED NUT BARS

Preparation time: 30 minutes
Baking time: 10 minutes

1 cup	graham cracker crumbs	250 mL
2 tbsp	sugar	30 mL
¼ cup	butter, melted	50 mL
2 cups	miniature marshmallows	500 mL
32	caramels	32
3 tbsp	milk	45 mL
½ cup	salted peanuts, coarsely chopped	125 mL

- Heat oven to 350°F (180°C). In medium bowl, stir together crumbs, sugar and butter. Press onto bottom of 9-inch (23 cm) square baking pan. Bake for 10 minutes.
- Sprinkle marshmallows over crust. In small saucepan, melt caramels with milk over low heat, stirring occasionally, until melted (9 to 12 minutes).
- Drizzle mixture over marshmallows; sprinkle with peanuts. Refrigerate until firm.

15 bars

NUTRITION FACTS (1 bar)
Calories 220 • Protein 3 g • Carbohydrate 31 g
Fat 10 g • Cholesterol 15 mg • Sodium 180 mg

SIMPLE FUDGY SAUCEPAN BROWNIES

Preparation time: 15 minutes
Baking time: 25 minutes
Cooling time: 30 minutes

BROWNIES

½ cup	butter	125 mL
2	squares (1 oz/28 g each) unsweetened baking chocolate	2
1 cup	sugar	250 mL
¾ cup	all-purpose flour	175 mL
2	eggs	2

FROSTING

¼ cup	butter	50 mL
3 tbsp	milk	45 mL
1	square (1 oz/28 g) unsweetened baking chocolate	1
2½ cups	powdered sugar	625 mL
½ tsp	vanilla	2 mL

- Heat oven to 350°F (180°C). In large saucepan, combine ½ cup (125 mL) butter and 2 squares chocolate. Cook over medium heat, stirring constantly, until melted (3 to 5 minutes). Stir in all remaining brownie ingredients until well mixed.
- Spread into greased 9-inch (23 cm) square baking pan. Bake for 25 to 30 minutes or until brownies begin to pull away from sides of pan.
- In same saucepan, combine ¼ cup (50 mL) butter, milk and 1 square chocolate; bring to a full boil. Remove from heat. Add powdered sugar; beat until smooth. Stir in vanilla.
- Frost brownies while warm. Let cool and cut into squares.

16 brownies

NUTRITION FACTS (1 brownie)
Calories 240 • Protein 2 g • Carbohydrate 34 g
Fat 12 g • Cholesterol 50 mg • Sodium 100 mg

APPLE PUFF PASTRY TART

Preparation time: 20 minutes
Baking time: 35 minutes

PASTRY

½	package (17¼ oz/489 g – 1 sheet) frozen puff pastry, thawed	½

FILLING

3 to 4	tart medium apples, peeled, cored, sliced ¼-inch (5 mm)	3 to 4
½ cup	sugar	125 mL
⅓ cup	flaked coconut	75 mL
⅓ cup	chopped pecans	75 mL
¼ cup	butter, melted	50 mL
¼ cup	raisins	50 mL
1½ tsp	cinnamon	7 mL

- Heat oven to 350°F (180°C). On lightly floured surface, roll out pastry to 13 x 9-inch (33 x 23 cm) rectangle. Place in greased 13 x 9-inch (33 x 23 cm) baking pan; prick with fork.
- Arrange apples on top of pastry. In small bowl, stir together all remaining ingredients; sprinkle over apples. Bake for 35 to 40 minutes or until apples are tender. Serve warm.

10 servings

NUTRITION FACTS (1 serving)
Calories 260 • Protein 2 g • Carbohydrates 31 g
Fat 16 g • Cholesterol 20 mg • Sodium 140 mg

BLUEBERRY SOUR CREAM PIE

Preparation time: 15 minutes
Baking time: 10 minutes
Cooling time: 30 minutes
Chilling time: 1 hour

CRUST

1½ cups	graham cracker crumbs	375 mL
⅓ cup	butter, melted	75 mL

FILLING

1 cup	light *or* fat free sour cream	250 mL
1¼ cups	fat free skim milk	300 mL
1	package (3½ oz/99 g) vanilla instant pudding and pie filling mix*	1
1 cup	fresh blueberries**	250 mL

- Heat oven to 350°F (180°C). In medium bowl, stir together crumbs and butter. Press onto bottom and sides of 9-inch (23 cm) pie pan. Bake for 10 to 12 minutes or until lightly browned. Let cool completely.

- In small mixer bowl, place sour cream. Beat at medium speed, gradually adding milk, until smooth (1 to 2 minutes). Continue beating, gradually adding pudding and scraping bowl often, until well mixed and thickened (1 to 2 minutes).

- Pour into baked crust. Refrigerate until set (1 to 2 hours). Top with blueberries.

** Substitute 1 package (0.9 oz/25 g) sugar-free vanilla instant pudding and pie filling.*

*** Substitute your favorite fresh fruit.*

8 servings

NUTRITION FACTS (1 serving)
Calories 240 • Protein 4 g • Carbohydrate 32 g
Fat 11 g • Cholesterol 28 mg • Sodium 420 mg

Orange Nut Butter Cake

Preparation time: 30 minutes
Baking time: 50 minutes
Cooling time: 1 hour

Cake

1 cup	sugar	250 mL
¾ cup	butter, softened	175 mL
3	eggs	3
1 tbsp	grated orange peel	15 mL
1 tsp	vanilla	5 mL
1 cup	orange marmalade	250 mL
3 cups	all-purpose flour	750 mL
1 tsp	baking soda	5 mL
½ tsp	baking powder	2 mL
½ tsp	salt	2 mL
⅓ cup	orange juice	75 mL
1	can (5 oz/148 mL) evaporated milk	1
1 cup	chopped walnuts	250 mL

Glaze

1 cup	powdered sugar	250 mL
1 tbsp	butter, softened	15 mL
½ tsp	grated orange peel	2 mL
2 to 3 tbsp	orange juice	30 to 45 mL

- Heat oven to 350°F (180°C). In large mixer bowl, combine sugar and ¾ cup (175 mL) butter. Beat at medium speed, scraping bowl often, until creamy (1 to 2 minutes). Continue beating, adding eggs one at a time, beating well after each addition until well mixed (1 to 2 minutes). Reduce speed to low; add orange peel, vanilla and orange marmalade. Beat until well mixed (1 minute).
- In medium bowl, combine flour, baking soda, baking powder and salt. Gradually add flour mixture alternately with orange juice and evaporated milk to butter mixture until well blended (1 to 2 minutes). By hand, stir in chopped nuts.
- Spoon into greased and floured 10-inch (25 cm) tube pan. Bake for 50 to 60 minutes or until toothpick inserted in center comes out clean. Let cool in pan 10 minutes; remove from pan. Let cool completely.
- In small mixer bowl, combine all glaze ingredients *except* orange juice. Beat at low speed, scraping bowl often and gradually adding enough orange juice for desired glazing consistency. Glaze cooled cake.

16 servings

NUTRITION FACTS (1 serving)
Calories 370 • Protein 6 g • Carbohydrate 54 g
Fat 16 g • Cholesterol 70 mg • Sodium 280 mg

BEST BUTTER CAKE WITH BROWNED BUTTER FROSTING

Preparation time: 20 minutes
Baking time: 25 minutes
Cooling time: 30 minutes

CAKE

⅔ cup	butter, softened	150 mL
⅔ cup	sugar	150 mL
2	eggs	2
2 tsp	vanilla	10 mL
2 cups	all-purpose flour	500 mL
1 tbsp	baking powder	15 mL
¼ tsp	salt	1 mL
1 cup	milk	250 mL

FROSTING

¼ cup	butter	50 mL
3 cups	powdered sugar	750 mL
2 tsp	vanilla	10 mL
3 to 4 tbsp	milk	45 to 60 mL

- Heat oven to 350°F (180°C). In large mixer bowl, combine ⅔ cup (150 mL) butter and sugar. Beat at medium speed, scraping bowl often, until creamy (1 to 2 minutes). Add eggs and vanilla. Continue beating, scraping bowl often, until well mixed (1 minute).
- Reduce speed to low. Beat, gradually adding flour, baking powder and salt alternately with milk and scraping bowl often, until well mixed (1 to 2 minutes).
- Divide batter between 2 greased and floured 8 or 9-inch (20 or 23 cm) round cake pans. Bake for 25 to 30 minutes or until toothpick inserted in center comes out clean. Let cool 5 minutes; remove from pans. Let cool completely.
- Meanwhile, in small saucepan, melt ¼ cup (50 mL) butter over medium-low heat until lightly browned (4 to 5 minutes).
- Transfer butter to small mixer bowl; add powdered sugar and vanilla. Beat at medium speed, scraping bowl often and gradually adding enough milk for desired spreading consistency. Spread frosting between cooled cake layers, top and sides of cake.

TIP: Cake can be baked in 13 x 9-inch (33 x 23 cm) baking pan. Bake for 30 to 35 minutes.

16 servings

NUTRITION FACTS (1 SERVING)
Calories 290 • Protein 3 g • Carbohydrate 44 g
Fat 12 g • Cholesterol 55 mg • Sodium 250 mg

CHOCOLATE CHUNK COOKIES

Preparation time: 30 minutes
Baking time: 9 minutes

1 cup	butter, softened	250 mL
¾ cup	firmly packed brown sugar	175 mL
½ cup	sugar	125 mL
1	egg	1
1½ tsp	vanilla	7 mL
2¼ cups	all-purpose flour	550 mL
1 tsp	baking soda	5 mL
½ tsp	salt	2 mL
1 cup	coarsely chopped walnuts	250 mL
1	milk chocolate candy bar (8 oz /225 g) cut into ½-inch (1 cm) pieces	1

- Heat oven to 375°F (190°C). In large mixer bowl, combine butter, brown sugar, sugar, egg and vanilla. Beat at medium speed, scraping bowl often, until well mixed (1 to 2 minutes).
- Reduce speed to low; add flour, baking soda and salt. Beat, scraping bowl often, until well mixed (1 to 2 minutes). By hand, stir in walnuts and chocolate.
- Drop dough by rounded tablespoonfuls 2 inches (5 cm) apart onto cookie sheets. Bake for 9 to 11 minutes or until lightly browned. Cool 1 minute; remove from pans.

3 dozen

NUTRITION FACTS (1 cookie)
Calories 160 • Protein 2 g • Carbohydrate 18 g
Fat 9 g • Cholesterol 20 mg • Sodium 125 mg

RASPBERRY BAVARIAN CREAM

Preparation time: 15 minutes
Cooking time: 7 minutes
Cooling time: 30 minutes
Chilling time: 2 hours

1 cup	milk	250 mL
1	envelope (¼ oz/7 g) unflavored gelatin	1
2 tbsp	water	30 mL
½ cup	sugar	125 mL
1 cup	light sour cream	250 mL
½ tsp	almond extract	2 mL
1	package (10 oz/284 g) frozen raspberries in syrup, thawed	1

- In medium saucepan, heat milk over medium heat until it just comes to a boil (5 to 7 minutes). In small bowl, sprinkle gelatin over water; let stand 5 minutes.
- Add gelatin mixture and sugar to milk; stir until dissolved. Let cool to room temperature (30 minutes).
- With wire whisk, stir in sour cream and almond extract until smooth. Pour into 1-quart (1 L) mold. Cover and refrigerate until set (2 to 3 hours).
- Unmold onto serving plate; top with raspberries. Cover and store refrigerated.

8 servings

NUTRITION FACTS (1 serving)
Calories 120 • Protein 3 g • Carbohydrate 22 g
Fat 2 g • Cholesterol 5 mg • Sodium 40 mg

Index